Moving Forward with Care

Community Care Services For Older People in Angus, Dundee City and Perth & Kinross

Social Work Services Inspectorate for Scotland

1996

Purpose and responsibilities

Our purpose is to work with others to continually improve social work services so that:

- they genuinely meet people's needs; and
- the public has confidence in them.

The Social Work Services Inspectorate
James Craig Walk
Edinburgh
EH1 3BA

SECRETARY OF STATE

You asked me to inspect community care services in Angus, Dundee and Perth & Kinross. This is my report.

In order to complete the report timeously we have focused our attention on services for older people which comprise nearly 90% of community care services. We anticipate that our findings and conclusions will be of interest to all agencies involved in delivering community care services across Scotland.

The Inspection Team, all of whom maintained their other duties during this period, focused their abilities and energies very effectively to complete the inspection and report on time. The Inspection Team was led by Assistant Chief Inspector Gillian Ottley and included SWS Inspectors John Bishop, Rosemary Bland, and Val Cox. They were assisted by Marc Mazzucco of Price Waterhouse and Katie Quinn (Research Assistant). Ms Anja Amsel was the Lay Member of the Inspection Team. Anna Thomson of SWSI provided the administrative support throughout. Each has made a contribution of excellence reflecting their professional skill and personal commitment to moving forward community care services in the best interests of service users.

Throughout the inspection we have received every co-operation from Angus, Dundee City and Perth & Kinross Councils and their staff, from private sector agencies and associations and from voluntary sector bodies. Their skills and commitment match those of the inspection team and I am grateful to them. We all share the common objective of continuously improving social work services.

This report contributes to that objective. It deals with important elements in the vital partnerships between social work and health agencies, between purchasers and providers and between government and local authorities. Our greatest concern is that too often users of community care services – in this case mainly older people – are not seen as partners but as recipients or, almost, supplicants. Far from empowering them the systems seem to dis-empower them through assessment processes they and their carers often have little say in, financial systems they frequently do not understand and decisions about arrangements for their care which they experience not as choices but as the least troublesome option for others.

I trust that all who consider the report keep the needs and strengths of older people and other users of community care services as their first priority.

Angus Skinner
Chief Social Work Inspector
31st October 1996

CONTENTS

Foreword I

Introduction 1

Angus Council 7
- Needs and provision for older people 8
- Existing provision of community care services for older people 8
- The Quality of Care in Residential and Nursing Homes in Angus 11
- The Frailty of Older People Living in Residential and Nursing Homes in Angus 15
- Costs of community care services 16
- Comparative Costs and Potential Savings 18
- Planning and purchasing 20
- Impact of regulation and charging 22
- The views of service users in Angus 23

Dundee City Council 27
- Needs and provision for older people 28
- Existing provision of community care services for older people 28
- The Quality of Care in Residential and Nursing Homes in Dundee City 31
- The Frailty of Older People living in Residential and Nursing Homes in Dundee City 34
- Costs of community care services 35
- Comparative Costs and Potential Savings 37
- Planning and purchasing 39
- Impact of regulation and charging 41
- The views of service users in Dundee 42

Perth & Kinross Council 45
- Needs and provision for older people 45
- Existing Provision Of Community Care Services For Older People 46
- The Quality of Care in Residential and Nursing Homes in Perth & Kinross 50
- The Frailty of Older People living in Residential and Nursing Homes in Perth & Kinross. 54
- Costs of community care services 55
- Comparative Costs and Potential Savings 57
- Planning and purchasing 59
- Impact of regulation and charging 61
- The views of service users in Perth & Kinross 62

Conculsions and Recommendations 67
- Quality of care and Standards 67
- Value for money 70
- The planning, provision and purchasing of services 73
- Information 77
- Comments By Lay Member 81
- Recommendations for Angus Council 84
- Recommendations for Dundee City Council 86
- Recommendations for Perth & Kinross Council 88
- Recommendation for Tayside Health Board 90
- Recommendations for The Scottish Office 91

Appendix 1
- Matching The Needs Of, And Provision For, Older People Aged 75+ i

Appendix 2
- Notes To Costs Analysis viii

Appendix 3
- Local Authority Costings x

Appendix 4
- The Quality Of Care In Residential Care Homes And Nursing Homes xvii

Foreword

This report presents findings and recommendations from our inspection of the provision and purchasing of community care services in Angus, Dundee and Perth & Kinross which was carried out between July 1996 and October 1996. This inspection was announced on 29th May, 2 months after local government reorganisation. It took place at a time when many of the new Councils were beginning anew to consider issues to do with the balance of care, value for money, and the efficiency and effectiveness of their social work services.

Our remit was:

to examine the arrangements for the provision and purchase of community care services in Angus, Dundee and Perth & Kinross;

to assess the effectiveness of these local authorities' approach to ensuring value for money in their provision and purchase of services;

to evaluate the efficiency with which the services are delivered;

to make recommendations.

We looked in particular at the needs of older people.

The Inspection had the following components.

We interviewed a sample of older people in Angus, Dundee, and Perth & Kinross who were in a residential or nursing home or used domiciliary care services; where the older person had problems with their memory we consulted their family carer. We commissioned an independent market research agency to assist us with this.

We invited the local authorities, the Health Board and the local health service trusts, the private sector organisations and the voluntary sector bodies to submit any information relevant to our remit and studied all that they submitted.

We considered the relevant national and local statistics relating to community care services. We analysed the information provided to us by the local authorities on the costs of their provision and purchase of community care services.

We examined several issues more closely through interviews with:

the Directors of Social Work and their senior managers in the three authorities concerned;

the Director of Commissioning and Strategic Management for Tayside Health Board;

the Director of Social Work for The Church of Scotland.

We met with private sector providers of residential homes, nursing homes and domiciliary care to hear their views at first hand.

We gave officials in each authority and the health board an opportunity to comment on the factual accuracy of a draft report.

The report starts with a brief introduction about community care. In Chapters 2, 3 and 4 we describe the position in Angus, Dundee, and Perth & Kinross. In each authority we have:

estimated the needs, and mapped the provision of care services for older people;

examined indicators of quality of care, and the frailty of older residents in residential and nursing homes;

reviewed and analysed the prices and costs of independent sector and local authority care for older people;

reviewed the existing community care plan, the joint planning procedures and purchasing policies for service;

examined the impact of regulation and charging policies on community care services;

surveyed the experience and views of a sample of older people about the information that was made available to them about the service they were receiving.

In Chapter 5 we draw together our conclusions and recommendations. Anja Amsel's independent comments are annexed to this chapter.

Introduction

1 Community care covers a wide range of services. In Scotland at 31 March 1995 there were 15,325 older people who were resident in a local authority or registered care home or who used a care home for holiday or respite care.[1] 14,807 older people were resident in nursing homes and private hospitals.[2] Over 15,000 older people also used day centres and many more relied on home care which embraces a wide number of services: the home help service, the provision of meals on wheels, community alarms, occupational therapy support and, more recently, social care officers.[3] The warden service allied to sheltered housing is also an important component of home care.

2 Because rates of disability and dependency increase with old age, older people are one of the most vulnerable groups of people in our society and their numbers are increasing. In Scotland, the number of older people aged 85 and over, who are the main users of community care services, increased by over 60% between 1980 and 1994. Their numbers are expected to rise further to reach a peak of over 90,000 by 2001.

3 The last fifteen years has seen an increase in the provision of all care services across Scotland to meet the needs of this increasing population. Between 1980 and 1995:

- the number of beds in all residential care homes rose to 16,988, having reached a peak of 18,346 in 1990;
- the number of beds in private nursing homes increased by 14,173 (almost 300%) to 19,236. In 1987 there were 6.7 nursing home beds for every 1000 people aged 65 or over; by 1995 there were 24.9 beds for every 1000 people aged 65 or over;
- the number of people receiving a home help increased by over 55%;
- the number of places in day centres increased by 137%;
- the number of sheltered housing dwellings increased by over 300%.

4 In relation to the needs of older people, the Government's expectation is that local authorities should "give special emphasis to the development of domiciliary and day care services as an alternative to residential care".[4] Moving to a care home is a major decision for most older people and should only occur after careful assessment has established that this is the best course of action. It is a decision older people should only be asked to make once.

5 Research literature[5] reiterates the stressful effect on all human beings of moving from one environment to another. Particular groups of people who are at greatest risk include people with "a marked degree of brain failure" (such as in moderate to severe dementia), severe physical illness or frailty. Older people with such frailties are at high risk of not being able to adjust successfully if they have to move. A move is also likely to have negative outcomes for people who experience the move as being abandoned, separated or rejected.

6 After their needs have been assessed older people should have as much choice as possible about how they are met. Every effort should be made to inform older people and

their carers about the possible choices available to them. Often this choice may be limited since the local authority may have already made certain decisions about the range of services it can support, or a person's choice may be limited by their needs, e.g. poor health, or by their circumstances, e.g. the charges they or their family may face.

7 As previously stated in our Introduction to the Lanarkshire inspection, "Assessment and choice are central issues in the development of community care services. Local authorities operate within fixed budgets and must decide how best to use these resources to meet the needs of their populations. They need to know about the range and quality of services currently available from providers in the area, and they need good quality information about current and projected levels and types of need within their population. In co-operation with health and housing services, they are required to plan for the provision of services to meet the range of identified and anticipated need within their authority, within the financial resources available to them. To do this, they must make choices, including choices about what services to purchase, for how many people, at what cost. These choices themselves limit the choices available to those responsible for assessing individual's needs and, indeed to those individuals themselves."

8 In the 1980s older people were not assessed before being admitted to private or voluntary residential or nursing homes. If they could not meet the costs themselves, the fees were paid by the Department of Social Security. The Government was concerned that this was leading to unnecessary growth in residential and nursing care, because some older people might have preferred to stay at home had it been possible to provide them with sufficient help.

9 It was to tackle these problems that the Government introduced new arrangements for community care services in 1993. The lead role was given to local authorities who, in conjunction with others (Health Boards and Housing), were charged with planning care in the community, assessing people's needs, and providing them with the best care they could.

10 This inspection involved estimating the needs and mapping the provision of care services for older people within the 3 Councils concerned. In order to estimate needs we used Isaacs'[6] model of intervals of need. This model is one way of reaching a conclusion about whether the response of care services matches the needs of older people. It is explained in detail at Appendix 1. It is only one model amongst many. Other useful techniques for assessing the aggregate needs of populations can be found in our publication 'Population Needs Assessment in Community Care'[7] published earlier this year.

11 Community care is not only about meeting the needs of older people by providing the services they require. Money is also a major consideration and when demands on services are set to increase it is vital that the available money is used efficiently. This inspection also involved assessing the full cost to the 3 Councils of providing residential care, day care and home care for older people within the respective geographic areas. The cost calculations were based on current COSLA/CIPFA guidance, where appropriate, and all figures on which the calculations are based were submitted by the Councils; it is emphasised that the figures submitted (Appendix 3) have not been subjected to any review or audit.

12 We also looked at the frailty of older people in different residential settings across sectors and we have sought to compare the quality of care that exists within different

homes. Some have argued, particularly in local authorities, that the quality of care in local authority homes is reflected in their higher costs. Private providers have argued that they provide better value for money: that is, they can provide good quality care for people with similar dependencies at a lower cost than that incurred by the local authorities.

13 In 1994/95 gross expenditure by Scottish local authorities on community care for older people was £400m. Residential homes expenditure increased by 21% over the previous year to £167m., brought about by the continuing shift in financial responsibility for residential care from the DSS to local authorities.[8] The gross expenditure on community care, for all care groups, by local authorities in Scotland in 1996/97 will be about £700m. Figures provided by the local authorities to SWSG suggest that services to older people will account for £500 million of this.

14 The responsibilities of the new councils were not quite the same as the responsibilities of the old authorities. Some responsibilities such as sewerage, river purification, Further Education Bursaries and Travel, and the Children's Reporter service were transferred from the old authorities to new agencies rather than to the new councils. Comparing the level of funding available to the new councils as opposed to the old has to take account of these changes.

15 Each year the Government estimates the amount of expenditure by local authorities which it is prepared to support through grant; this is called Grant Aided Expenditure (GAE). The GAE for the predecessor authorities for 1995-96 was £404.5 million. The responsibilities transferred to new agencies rather than to the new councils of Angus, Dundee City and Perth & Kinross amounted (according to the best estimate we have been able to obtain) to some £15 million. The GAE for 1996-97 for the responsibilities which the new councils inherited can therefore be estimated as £389.5 million. The new councils have two areas of increased responsibility compared with their predecessors. These are for the costs of local government re-organisation (estimated at £3.4 million) and for further transfer of community care responsibilities (estimated at £2.8 million). Taking account of all of these changes we may estimate that to match the GAE of their predecessors the new councils total GAE should be £395.7 million. The GAE for the new councils for 1996-97 is £400 million, 1.1% above the base estimated. However, the councils have also had to meet wage and price increases from within this allocation. Taking this into account it can be seen that the resources available to the councils have decreased marginally in real terms.

16 Within this overall context it is for each local Council to determine their priorities and allocate resources within the expenditure limit imposed by the Secretary of State's tax capping regime. The GAE estimates for each service are therefore only indicative. Table 1 below shows the GAE estimates for social work services for the 3 new Councils and for the former Tayside Region. This shows that whilst the overall GAE for social work remained virtually unchanged (£75.1 million in 1996-97 compared with £75 million in 1995-96) there were significant differences between the elements for community care funding and those for the rest of the social work services. The GAE for community care services increased by £2.8 million (transfer referred to above) but other elements in the overall assessment of community care services fell by £0.8 million, giving an overall increase of £2

million. The GAE for other social work services fell from £22.4 million to £20.5 million, a fall of £1.9 million. In short, whilst the social work GAE contained an increase of £2.8 million for additional community care responsibilities, it also contained a reduction of £2.7 million.

Council/Region	Community Care (£m)	Other Social Work (£m)	All Social Work (£m)
Angus	16.1	4.7	20.8
Dundee City	21.7	10.6	32.3
Perth & Kinross	16.8	5.2	22.0
Total New Councils 1996-97	54.6	20.5	75.1
Tayside 1995-96	52.6	22.4*	75.0*
Change 1996-97 from 1995-96	**Increase of £2 million**	**Decrease of -£1.9 million**	**Increase of £0.1 million**

* *Adjusted to take account of the fact that from 1 April 1996 Councils were no longer responsible for Reporters to Children's Panels.*

Table 1: Comparative GAE Estimates 1995-96 and 1996-97 for Angus, Dundee City, Perth & Kinross and Former Tayside Region

17 All the new Councils have found it necessary to introduce charges for non-residential care services. Without the introduction of charges the social work departments would have been required to make cuts in the service or alternative savings. The Government's general policy on charges for local services is that those able to meet all or part of the economic cost should be expected to do so. Effective costing and charging procedures can be valuable in achieving the best use of resources across the range of personal social services, and social work departments are expected to develop them. In a context of increasing demand and reducing budgets ensuring value for money in the provision of services to older people is and needs to remain a continuing concern if managers are to be able to deploy resources effectively.

18 The Government's White Paper, "Caring for People" advocated linking care management with delegated responsibility for budgetary management. This was considered to be an important way of enabling those closest to the identification of client needs to make the best possible use of the resources available. Recent research from Stirling University[9] supports this view. Researchers found that, once a decision had been taken to support someone in their own home, devolved responsibility for resource allocation assisted needs-led care planning.

19 To encourage local authorities to plan their community care expenditure and to seek value for money from all the services they purchase, the Secretary of State issued Directions on Purchasing which came into effect in December 1994. These Directions required authorities to set out in their community care plans the types and volumes of services which they anticipated purchasing and the level of expenditure which they planned to allocate to each of the sectors (voluntary, private, local authority). The White Paper acknowledged that Scottish local authorities were likely to remain major providers of care "for the time being", but stated that they should "promote and make greater use of the facilities of the voluntary and private sector, taking account of the different circumstances

in different parts of Scotland". Since the Community Care Act in 1990 and its implementation from 1993 onwards, the balance of residential care in Scotland continues to shift, albeit slowly, from local authorities to the independent sector. At 31 March 1996, 48% of beds for older people in residential care were in local authority homes and 52% were in independent sector homes (27% private sector and 25% voluntary sector).[10]

20 At the heart of this inspection we examined questions about the effectiveness with which each of the three Councils were taking forward their strategic responsibilities for ensuring that their service users benefited from the best services the authority could provide or obtain, within the constraints of their budget and the numbers of users whose needs they had to meet.

Chapter 2

Angus Council

1 Angus, with a population of 110,000 people, is a mainly rural area to the North and East of Dundee. There are 7 principal towns, Monifieth, Carnoustie, Arbroath and Montrose on the coast, with Brechin, Forfar and Kirriemuir inland. There is no natural centre to the area. This geography, and the shape of health service provision, has influenced the thinking about the development of community care services.

2 At the present time Angus Council and Angus National Health Service Trust have established three "geographically-based responsibility centres" on which community care services are based. The localities are: Arbroath/Carnoustie/Monifieth; Forfar/Kirriemuir/South-West Angus, and; Montrose/Brechin. Each locality has a service manager responsible for most community care services. The Social Work Department also operates a fourth responsibility centre which provides a specialist service, on an Angus-wide basis, to adults with mental health problems, to those who misuse drugs or alcohol, and those with HIV infection or AIDS.

3 In relation to each of the community care user groups, Angus Council makes available a range of residential and, where appropriate, nursing home care in addition to domiciliary, day and respite care services. Some of these services are provided directly by the council itself, other services are purchased from the private and voluntary sectors.

4 All day care for adults with learning disabilities is provided by the local authority, through its 3 Adult Resource Centres. The local authority is also a major provider of day care for adults with mental health problems, through the Day Access Rural Tayside (DART) programme. As at 30 September 1996 there are 80 places available at the DART Project programme of day care. There are also voluntary sector and health sector day centres for people with mental health problems. Day services in Angus are currently being reviewed as part of the development of the Angus Mental Health Strategy.

5 At present there is no Angus-based provision of specialist day care services for people with physical disabilities (including sensory impairment), or with substance misuse problems. The nearest available day care provision for these groups is in Dundee. Day care provision for people with physical disabilities is jointly commissioned with Dundee City Council and Perth & Kinross Council at the Mackinnon Centre in Dundee. This Centre also provides a respite care service for people with physical disabilities. The local authority resource centre at Seaton Grove caters for people with dementia on a day care, respite and long-term basis, and there is one local authority home which provides specialised residential care for people with dementia. There is no local authority residential provision in Angus for people with substance misuse problems.

6 The Community Care Action Plan for Angus estimates that within the area there are:

2,750 adults (age 16-64) with a severe or very severe physical disability;

350 adults with learning disabilities;

2,700 adults with a severe mental illness;

1,800 adults at high risk of alcohol dependency;

420 adults who are injecting drugs.

Needs and provision for older people

7 The Angus Council Community Care Plan estimates that in 1994 there were some 8,100 people over the age of 75 in Angus. This figure was based on data provided by the General Register Office (Scotland). Estimates from the same source indicate that the number of older people over 85 has increased to over 2,000 persons, compared to 1700 in 1990.

8 Using these data, and employing the Intervals of Need model developed by Isaacs,[11] we estimated that of all older people, aged 75 and above in Angus:

between 1,500 and 2,600 require intensive levels of support during the day and night;

between 225 and 900 require regular support several times a day;

between 1,000 and 2,200 require help solely with domestic tasks once a day or less.

The difference between the smaller and larger numbers depends on the amount of support older people obtain from their family, or other carers. If no families in Angus were prepared or able to support those older people who require intensive levels of support, 2,600 older people would have to obtain their support from public agencies.

Existing provision of community care services for older people

9 Older people requiring intensive support may obtain their support in either residential or community settings. Using the above figures based on Isaacs' model, and statistical information routinely provided to, or available to The Scottish Office, we estimated that for older people requiring intensive levels of support in Angus, in 1995/96:

a total of 319 "units of support"[12] were available, per 1000 people aged over 75 years;

over half the available provision was within hospital (144 places per 1000 people aged 75+);

residential and nursing homes provided most of the remaining provision (140 places per 1000 people aged 75+);

relatively few people received intensive support at home (34 people per 1000 received a home help service 6 or 7 days per week).

10 These figures suggest that community care services for older people in Angus who need intensive support, are currently largely hospital-based, with little community provision. There are few social care officers, or home help staff providing the intensive support older people and their families may require.

11 The same data suggest that some older people with a need for regular support during the day may experience difficulty in obtaining a range of appropriate support. Although sheltered housing with warden assistance is widely available, and day care provision is above the national average, the home help service is provided to only half the people in this group on more than 2 days a week. The provision of meals, community alarms and aids to daily living are also nearer the national average. Nursing support appears to be widely available, although below the Scottish average.

12 On the basis of these figures, it seems that the people who are best served by existing community care services in Angus, are those older people who require assistance with domestic tasks only. For example, over 80% of users of the home help service receive less than 4 hours of support per week, and in many cases this is likely to involve support for those who need assistance with household tasks, shopping and the collection of pensions.

Residential and nursing home care

13 Table 2 below shows the places in residential and nursing homes when Angus Council took over responsibility on 1st April 1996.

	No of Beds	Percent of Total	Occupancy (%)	Scotland (%)
Residential Homes				
Local Authority	200	18%	83	91
Private	325	29%	84	88
Voluntary	71	6%	97	92
Nursing Homes	541	48%	88	85
Total	1137	101%		

Table 2: Residential and Nursing Home Beds in Angus on 1st April 1996.

14 Local Authority residential home beds comprised 18% of the available bed spaces. The new Council was concerned that the staffing numbers in its own homes fell below the registration standards it had adopted. In order to increase the staffing ratios in local authority homes, the Council moved swiftly to reduce the number of beds in each home. It closed 32 beds (16% of its total). The number of residential and nursing home beds within the area at 1 September 1996 is shown in Table 3. Beds in local authority residential homes in Angus now comprise 15% of the available bed spaces.

	No of Beds	Percent of Total
Residential Homes		
Local Authority	168	15%
Private	340	30%
Voluntary	72	6%
Nursing Homes	540	48%
Total	1120	99%

Table 3: Residential and Nursing Home Beds in Angus on 1st September 1996.

15 There has been a decline in local authority beds for older people across Scotland during the last 10 years. Across all providers (local authority, private and voluntary sectors) the number of residential beds has recently shown a decrease, due in large part to conversion to single rooms in existing homes. In contrast to residential homes, bed spaces in Scottish nursing homes have almost quadrupled in the last decade. Angus has reflected this trend.

16 In Angus at present, the occupancy rates of local authority residential homes, that is the number of residents compared to the number of beds, are around 90%, due to the decrease in the number of available bed spaces. Occupancy rates in nursing homes are continuing to fall, since although admission rates have increased slightly, the number of beds has increased at a faster rate.

17 Since 1 April 1996, Angus Council has been purchasing residential care in private and voluntary sector homes as well as placing people in local authority homes. The council has continued to purchase places in the nursing home sector. Table 4 below shows the most recent pattern of admission to residential and nursing home care.

	No of Beds	Percent of Total
Residential Homes		
Local Authority	8	14%
Private	15	27%
Voluntary	5	9%
Nursing Homes	28	50%
Total	56	100%

Table 4: Admissions to Residential and Nursing Home Care in Angus 1.4.96 to 18.7.96.

18 The use made of private residential and nursing homes by Angus Council has been the subject of complaint by private sector providers who claim that the local authority place people in local authority homes more readily. The above Table shows that out of a total of 56 placements since 1 April 1996, only 14% were to local authority residential homes, whilst a total of 77% went to the private sector (50% to private nursing homes and 27% to private residential homes).

Day care

19 Most day care for older people in Angus is provided by voluntary organisations and funded by Angus Council. Some day care is provided within the local authority resource centre, Seaton Grove. No day centres are run by the private sector. In April 1996 Angus Council introduced charging for the use of day centres, at a rate of £12 a day.

20 The 5 voluntary day centres are open weekdays between 10:00 a.m. and 4:00 p.m. providing one meal and a range of social activities. There are over 125 places available on a daily basis in the 5 centres. The average cost to Angus Council of each place for each day is £14.04.

21 Seaton Grove provides 12 day care places, 7 days-a week, including 2 meals a day. It is open for longer hours than the voluntary sector day centres, providing particular support for older people with dementia.

Home care

22 In May 1996 the home help service in Angus remained a service provided to many older people, but for few hours. Over 75% of older people received the service for 3 hours or less each week. The service was oriented mainly towards providing domestic support, compared to personal care. Less than 30% of people received personal care.

23 From information provided to us the provision of meals, both mobile and at lunch clubs appeared to be above the Scottish average, as did the number of community alarms. Occupational therapy support – through the provision of aids to daily living, and advice on adaptations – was of average provision. The introduction of social care officers is an important contribution to providing intensive care to people living at home. The provision of sheltered housing, together with medium dependency housing allows for provision for 10% of the population over 75.

The Quality of Care in Residential and Nursing Homes in Angus

Residential Care Homes

24 We examined 25 reports provided by Angus Council on residential homes in its area in order to reach some conclusions about the quality of care provided. Reports were received on 17 private sector homes (one of which is also registered as a nursing home with Tayside Health Board), the 2 voluntary homes in the area and the 6 local authority homes. Twenty reports relate to inspections carried out by the inspection unit of Tayside Regional Council. Five reports (one voluntary sector home and 4 private homes) were completed by the new inspection unit of Angus Council and therefore carried out since 1 April 1996. (See Appendix 4 for details of legislative context, standard setting and our approach to the analysis).

25 We also looked at 4 reports on nursing homes, provided by Tayside Health Board.

26 Figure 1 below, shows the average percentage of standards met by residential homes across the sectors. These percentages were calculated by taking the number of standards met as a proportion of the total number applied in each section of every inspection report and dividing the total by the number of homes in each sector. The total average was calculated by adding the number of standards met by the homes in each sector and expressing this as a percentage of the total number of standards. Overall, on the available data, the private sector homes met on average the highest percentage of standards.

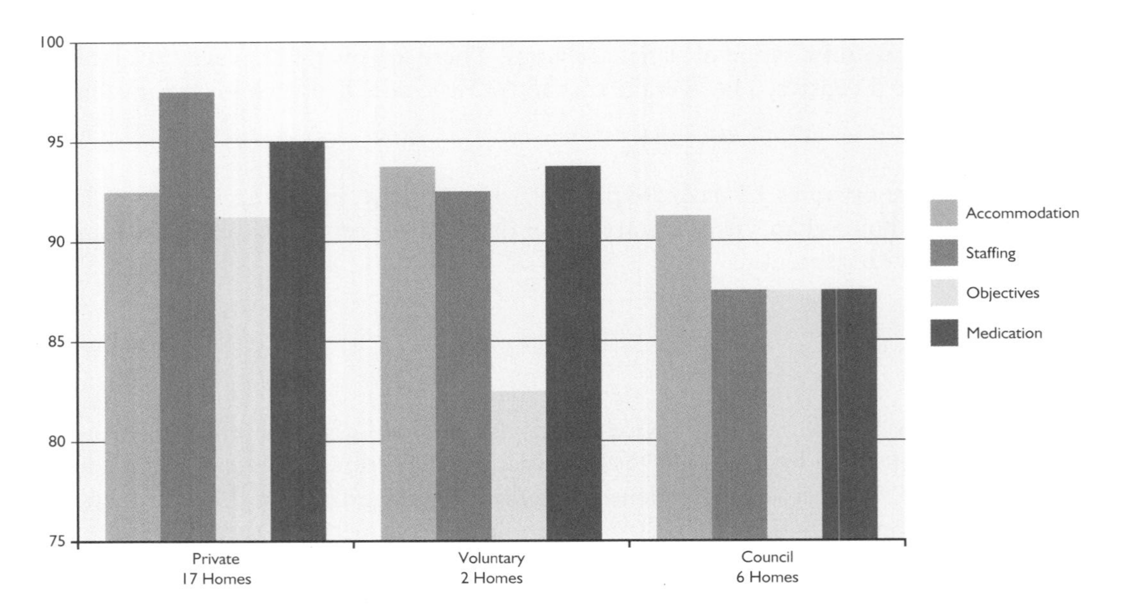

Figure 1: Average Percentage of Standards Met in Residential Homes by Sector in Angus.

27 Using the inspection reports available to us, our analysis showed that on average the local authority homes had previously met fewer of the required staffing standards than the independent sector homes. However, the new Council acted swiftly to remedy this situation by reducing the number of beds, thereby ensuring that the staffing ratios required by the standards were met in its own homes from 1st April 1996. Voluntary homes met 93% of the staffing standards on average and the private sector homes 97%. Night staffing requirements were met in all homes in each sector.

28 Lower staffing levels than those laid down in the standards for registration and inspection can have serious implications for the amount of care available to residents as well as the quality of care that a reduced staff group is able to give. Where lower than prescribed staff levels are combined with high levels of resident frailty, the potential for poor quality care and low staff morale arises.

29 Shortfalls in aspects of the accommodation included difficulty of access for disabled residents to various parts of the home or garden, the lack of call points throughout the home, and water temperature above or below a prescribed standard. Individual homes had not always carried out structural work called for in previous inspections, such as installation of a lift or providing additional sitting rooms or bathrooms, all of which have capital as well as revenue cost implications.

30 The reports showed a high level of standards met in relation to medication, apart from in the local authority homes. Nonetheless local inspectors criticised the quality of record-keeping in relation to medication procedures, resident contracts and written care plans. There was widespread evidence from local inspection unit interviews with a sample of residents that they were generally unaware of their rights, whether this concerned the written contract with the home, access to their care plan and their right to participate in its construction, or the right to a choice at mealtimes and to be consulted about menu planning generally.

ANGUS

31 Being able to make choices is as important to older people in homes as it is to everyone else. One very important choice is that of being able to choose not to share a bedroom with someone else. Figure 2 below shows that the Council homes offer significantly more choice in this regard. For all sectors the proportion of beds available as single rooms is high and reflects increasingly higher overall standards of provision in residential care.

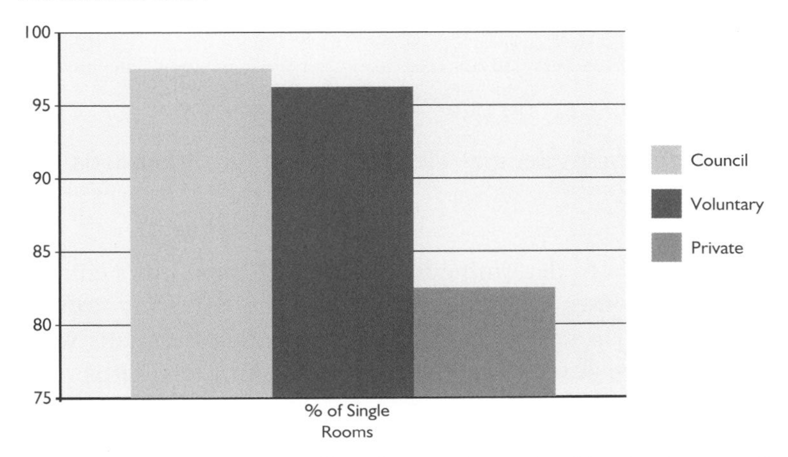

Figure 2: Percentage of Beds Available in Single Rooms By Sector in Angus.

32 Choices about planning your care and about menus and food are also important. We undertook a more detailed analysis on a sub-set of standards regarding the availability of these choices. We analysed the reports to compare the standards regarding older people's involvement in the construction of their care plans, whether their individual likes and dislikes about food were taken into account by homes and whether they were involved in or consulted about menu planning.

33 Table 5 below shows the number of homes which met the standards across the sectors.

Standard	Local Authority	Private	Voluntary
Care Plan involvement 2.28,2.31,2.32,2.35 or 2.36	Met in 5 out of 6 homes.	Met in 14 out of 17 homes.	Met in 1 out of 2 homes.
Menu Planning Involvement 2.60, 2.63,2.66,2.67,2.70, 2.71or 2.72.	Met in 3 out of 6 homes.	Met in 15 out of 17 homes.	Not met in either home.
Individual food preferences met 2.61,2.64,2.67,2.68, 2.71 2.72 or 2.73	Met in 5 out of 6 homes.	Met in all 17 homes.	Met in 1 out of 2 homes.

Note: The numbering given to the same standards varied between individual inspection reports, both within and across authorities. This is indicated at Column 1 of the Table.

Table 5: Proportion of Homes in Each Sector Meeting Selected Standards on Choices in Angus.

34 We examined the inspection reports to determine how local inspection units enforce the standards required of residential homes. Inspectors showed some flexibility around deadlines for shortfalls to be remedied: in some cases, where structural alterations were required, this was extended to up to three years. Some shortfalls in meeting standards were treated more seriously than others by inspectors. In some homes, standards were still unmet by the time a third inspection took place.

35 Angus Council adopted a new reporting format for annual inspection reports on 1st July 1996 which were intended to address quality of life issues more effectively as well as being easier to read. In addition the social work department has developed new quality service standards which are being piloted in the local authority's own homes. We examined the Council's new standards and found them to still be predominantly concerned with adherence to written procedures and with the existence of written policies. Few of the new 298 indicators relate to outputs, or to the outcomes of procedures or policies for residents. Many standards refer to staff first and residents second e.g. "Positive health measures for staff and residents will be promoted .... in line with departmental policies...", and tend to reinforce the regime which staff are expected to implement rather than emphasise the autonomy of residents.

Nursing Homes

36 In the reports on 4 Angus nursing homes, comments by Health Board inspectors regarding the quality of care ranged from 'favourable' to 'generally favourable'. The inspectors drew attention to shortfalls in aspects of the medication procedures and practice in all four nursing homes inspected. Other issues requiring attention included inadequate building and safety standards such as repairs to walls, inadequate lighting, worn carpets

and equipment. Suggestions were made about improving the attractiveness and decreasing the confusing aspects of the environment in one home where there was a high proportion of 'confused' residents.

37 Two of the 4 nursing homes inspected in Angus were found to have inadequate staffing levels and all 4 homes recorded a high number of minor accidents in the preceding 12 months (between 67 and 186), mostly consisting of falls, cuts and bruises. Occupancy levels were quite high in all these homes, ranging between 77% and 92%.

38 At present Tayside Health Board does not make Nursing Home inspection reports available to the local authority.

The Frailty of Older People Living in Residential and Nursing Homes in Angus

39 We were interested in comparing frailty levels in 2 distinct kinds of provision, residential homes and nursing homes, as well as between sectors. We used information about frailty in residential homes which is routinely submitted to The Scottish Office on an annual basis. We examined the data in relation to all local authority homes and a random, but broadly representative sample of homes run by private and voluntary organisations. Finally, we examined nursing home inspection reports provided to us by Tayside Health Board.

40 Our sample in Angus comprised 6 local authority residential homes, 7 private and 2 voluntary residential homes, and 4 nursing homes.

41 We looked at 3 types of frailty: incontinence; people who are bed or chair-bound; people who are "confused". The definition of "confusion" adopted by SWSG when requesting statistical returns from local authorities refers to people "whose mental confusion arises from brain pathology and is of permanent and irreversible nature, and who require regular supervision or help to perform tasks of daily living, or constant care because of aimless wandering etc." The definition of confusion used by medical staff when someone is admitted to a nursing home, or by a visiting member of an inspection team may be different.

42 In Angus, private sector homes care for some of the least and most frail residents. The voluntary homes have the lowest proportion of very frail residents. The local authority homes vary in the proportions of residents who are confused; two homes have specialist dementia units and one of these has a much higher proportion of confused residents than the remaining 5 homes. Figure 3 below shows that the nursing homes have high proportions of confusion and the highest levels of incontinence, although it is the private sector residential homes which have the highest proportion of residents who are bed or chairbound.

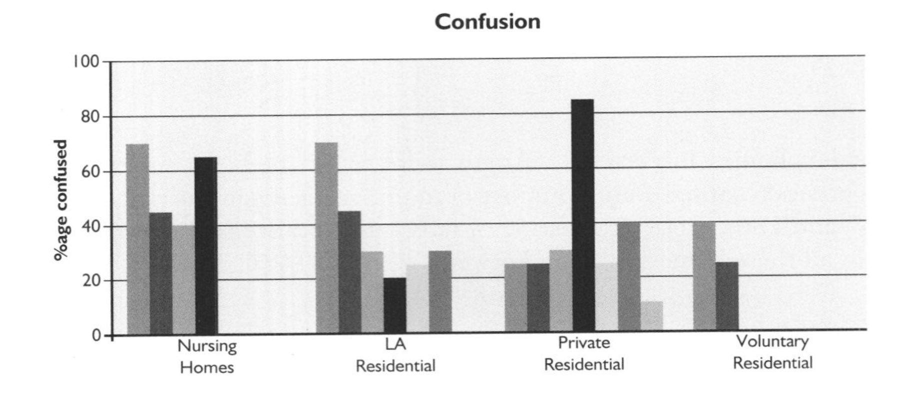

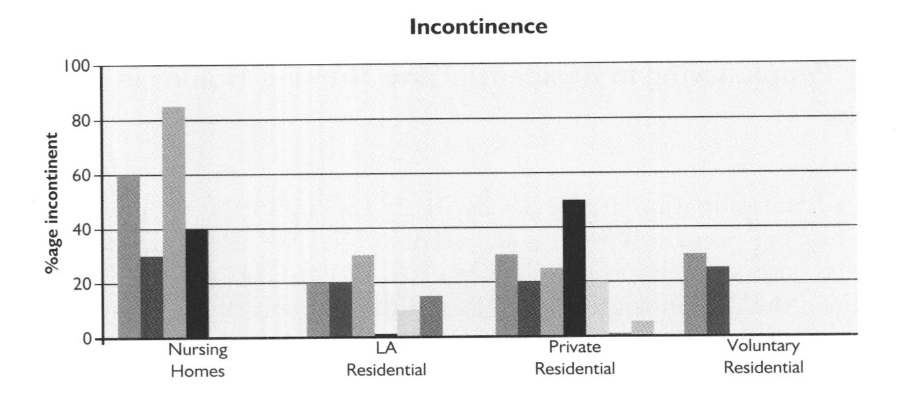

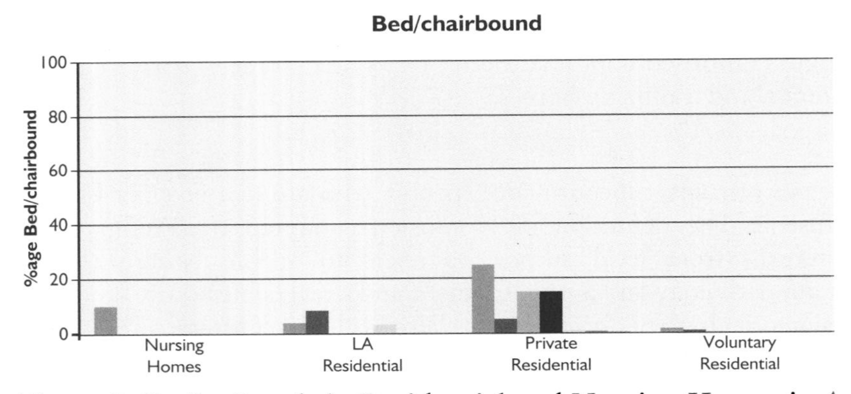

Figure 3: Frailty Levels in Residential and Nursing Homes in Angus.

COSTS OF COMMUNITY CARE SERVICES

Local Authority Residential Care

43 Angus Council runs 6 residential care homes. One home Seaton Grove provides both residential and day care, while the others, Beechhill, Camus, Fairlie, Lunan Park and St Drostan's provide residential care only. Seaton Grove and Beechhill also provide specialised residential care for people with dementia.

44 We calculated the actual costs of each of these homes, using figures supplied by the Council, and applying the current costing formula and guidance issued by COSLA and CIPFA, where appropriate. (See Appendix 2, Notes to Costs Analysis, and Appendix 3 for a full list of costs). We agreed with Angus Council Officers that we would use the average number (144) of long-term residents between 1 April 1996 and 31 August 1996 to enable us to calculate average weekly costs per resident.

45 The average weekly full cost varied in the different homes from a low of £364 per resident week to a high of £612 per resident week, with a weighted average weekly cost for all residents of £431. If the costs of the 2 dementia units are excluded then the average weekly costs range from a low of £318 to a high of £612, with a weighted weekly average of £410. The main reason for the divergence in costs between homes relates to the capital value of the buildings and occupancy levels.

46 The comparatively low cost of the least expensive home can be attributed to both occupancy (46 residents compared to an average of around 27) and also the fact that capital costs are split between the residential and day care facilities in this establishment.

47 Weekly average costs for the 2 dementia units varied from £579, to £660, with a weighted average weekly cost of £619.

48 It should also be noted that some of the costs currently included within the residential care costs relate to activities which are community-based, for example the provision of meals on wheels and the operational base for community alarm staff. Angus Council stated that it is currently working to improve the allocation of costs.

Domiciliary Care

49 The average cost per hour for the provision of domiciliary care within Angus is £6.25. Most of these costs relate to staff costs, which account for approximately 93% of care costs. However, with no overhead costs having been allocated by the Council to domiciliary care, the cost calculated is below the 'full cost'. The Angus Community Care Action Plan calculates the cost of domiciliary care as £6.50 per hour, based on costs to the former Tayside Regional Council.

Day Care

50 Day care is provided by the local authority at an average cost of £31.45 per care day. The day care centre opens 365 days a year, provides two meals each day and has longer opening hours than the average day centre, consequently the costs are fairly high. The cost of day care services is calculated as £22 per day in the Community Care Action Plan.

Performance against Standard Rate

51 Section 22 of the National Assistance Act 1948 requires local authorities to set a standard rate for local authority residential accommodation within their area. This amount should equate to the full cost to the authority of providing the care. Angus have performed against their published standard rate as follows:

	Standard Rate	Average Cost Calculated
Residential Care	£360.00/week	£410.28/week
Dementia Units	£570.00/week	£619.29/week

52 The Council's published standard rate for residential care is below the average full cost.

COMPARATIVE COSTS AND POTENTIAL SAVINGS

53 Currently, within Angus, independent sector providers are paid at a basic rate of £197 per week for residential care, although various premiums are added for different care packages. The figure of £230.48, used in the Table below, is the average cost paid to the independent sector by the local authority, taking account of these premiums. The original figures were supplied by the council.

54 Eligible residents placed in the independent sector receive from the Department of Social Security a Residential Allowance of £54.00 per week; this £54.00 is remitted to the local authority. No similar allowance is received by individuals placed in a local authority home. In addition, dependent on which sector the resident is in, a different level of income support is available. We have not included Attendance Allowances payable in the first four weeks, due to their marginal impact on costing.

55 Table 6 shows the costs to Angus Council of placing a resident in an independent sector home compared with the average costs of maintaining places in their own homes (excluding the higher costs of the special dementia units).

	Local Authority £	Independent £
Gross average cost per resident to local authority/price paid per resident by local authority	410.28	230.48
Less : Income received by local authority		
Residential Allowance	–	(54.00)
Income Support Premiums (Note 1[13])	–	(23.23)
Income Support (Note 2[14])	(48.00)	(34.15)
Net cost to local authority	**362.28**	**119.10**

Table 6: Comparative Costs to Angus Council of Local Authority Provision and Purchase from Independent Sector of Residential Care.

56 Table 6 shows that Angus Council could make savings by placing more residents in the independent sector. To identify the scale of the potential gross savings available to the local authority it is first necessary to consider costs that would not be saved. These fall into three areas.

57 First, some overhead costs and a proportion of the cost of capital would not be saved.

58 Secondly, the costs of effecting the closure of homes would need to be taken into account. Closure of local authority homes would either require redeployment of staff within the authority, or redundancies, or transfer to new providers. Each of these options would to some extent limit the savings which could be made. If homes were sold to private or voluntary sector providers the new owners might take on existing staff from the homes. These staff would, of course, be covered by the application of the Transfer of Undertakings (Protection of Employment) Regulations 1981, and it is possible, indeed likely, that new owners would be reluctant to accept such transfers.

59 The cost in the early years of closing or transferring homes to the independent sector might very substantially reduce the savings realised, particularly if redundancy costs all fell in the first year. In addition, and depending on the arrangements made, local authorities might not benefit from the £54 DSS income until the new provision had been established for some years.

60 Thirdly, a number of factors might contribute to rises in the price of places in the independent sector and thus further reduce the potential savings. To bring all the independent sector provision up to the standard of the Council's own provision in respect of single room accommodation would be likely to lead to price increases. Moreover it is arguable that the price charged to the Council by private and voluntary homes is artificially low and can only be sustained by higher charges made for privately financed placements and by some 'hidden costs' of services charged for particular services provided to individual residents. If the proportion of privately and publicly financed placements changed then arguably the charge to the Council could rise. Independent sector bodies have argued strongly that the prices paid by the Council are not sufficient.

61 It is not possible to quantify the effects of these diverse elements and a reasonable judgement must be made. It would be unrealistic for the Council to envisage that it could make savings proportionate to the variation in weekly cost given in Table 6. Nevertheless we consider that the Council could make more cost effective use of its resources by making significantly greater use of independent sector provision and that realistically the potential savings could be between £850,000 and £1.7 million which could be otherwise applied to enhance community care services[15].

62 These considerations point to ensuring that a realistic view is taken of potential savings and careful management of any changes. Managing any substantial change in services for vulnerable people requires great care on the part of the local authority and may only be achieved successfully over a period of time. The authority must plan its change strategy well, must allow sufficient time for implementation, and must communicate its intentions to service users and carers, to their own staff and to the wider public, in a way which is both informative and reassuring about the continuing care which will be available. This requires local authorities to make a realistic appraisal of the most cost-efficient mixed economy for their area, and to plan a strategy to achieve this within a realistic timescale.

63 Angus Council have made it clear that they believe it is important to retain local authority residential provision in order to provide choice and to maintain a mixed economy of care.

Budget Setting and Control

64 Our review of Angus Council's budgetary control mechanisms for 1996/97 identified that budgets had been incrementally set using as the base year a disaggregated Tayside Regional Council budget. Because there was a need to set a budget quickly for the new unitary council, incremental budget setting was again to be deployed for the 1997/98 budget. The main reason put forward for the continued use of this budget setting mechanism was the significant financial savings which the Social Work Department had to make. It was felt that these were better made at departmental level, rather than at individual cost centre level.

65 The purchase of residential and nursing home care is delegated to service managers, who monitor placements into the independent sector against an agreed number of placements. The overall budget levels are controlled centrally, and service managers must raise with their Head of Service any problems they encounter with these agreed limits. Some arrangement of this kind is clearly necessary if limited budgets are to be managed effectively. As new arrangements are brought in we would expect the Council to take forward plans for greater devolved budgetary provision.

66 We were informed that the continued development of the K2 computerised client database system will eventually lead to the alignment of current financial ledger and management information systems; however, this is unlikely to occur within the next four to five years.

PLANNING AND PURCHASING

67 The Community Care Action Plan (1996/97) for the Angus Council was revised by the former Tayside Regional Council on behalf of the new unitary authority. Information contained in the former Regional Council's Community Care Plan was disaggregated to the level of each of the unitary authorities.

68 The revised Action Plan for 1996/97 contains a large number of broad brush statements relating to proposed action, by a range of agencies (including housing), to achieve a series of key objectives for services for older people. It sets out the funding source for these proposals, where applicable, and provides some information about the nature and scale of the consultations on the draft plan. The Plan also provides statistical data and estimates of need in relation to services for older people.

69 The Action Plan does not provide a clear statement of the local authority's purchasing intentions, although it does provide information about the pattern of purchasing by Tayside Regional Council's Social Work Department in the preceding year. The rationale for this was said by Angus Council to be that the outgoing authority was not in a position to comment on the purchasing intentions of the new authority. Angus Council has told us that its new Community Care Plan for 1997-2000 will provide information on the authority's purchasing intentions.

70 Whilst the Action Plan provides a range of statistical data in relation to each of the community care service groups, the plan makes little attempt to relate assessed aggregate needs to current service provision, with a view to identifying service gaps and deficiencies. It does not provide detailed information about expected levels of service over the planning period, nor does it consistently provide measurable objectives and targets. It does not specifically relate the planned actions of the authority to the overall policy objectives for

community care as set out in the White Paper "Caring for People". Finally it does not contain clear outputs and outcomes in relation to the planned actions, nor does it provide information about the financial resources and assumptions underpinning the planning statements.

71 Some of these weaknesses were identified by senior officers during our interviews. The Director of Social Work, Mr Robertson, emphasised the importance of including specific and measurable targets for each service area and associated financial information in the 1997 -2000 Community Care Plan, on which the authority is currently working with its planning partners. He subsequently indicated that until recently it had been difficult to provide detailed financial information because of a lack of clarity about the resource transfer intentions of Tayside Health Board.

72 Another senior officer commented on the difficulty of identifying purchasing intentions in volume terms, due in part to financial uncertainties, although he also noted that this should not prevent the authority from stating its intentions. These financial uncertainties were said to be partly the result of the different time frames for the strategic and financial planning processes within the authority. We were advised that it was recognised that there was a need to examine the scope for bringing the 2 processes closer into alignment.

73 Not all current planning activity is encompassed within the Community Care Plan. The Angus Mental Health Strategy is another example of planning for community care. The plan seeks to address the needs of adults with a mental illness, including older people with dementia. In draft form at present, the Strategy provides an illustration of good practice in joint planning. The Strategy, which is led by the Health Board, has been the subject of widespread consultation with users, carers and staff of the agencies concerned. The plan provides a thorough aggregate needs assessment and sets out specific and measurable targets. The £343,000 resource transfer for 1996/97 has been identified as the funding source for these targets. When we interviewed Mr Robertson he also described current work on a draft strategy for older people within Angus. Tayside Health Board anticipates that £19m will be transferred to the three authorities during the current 4-year programme. This will allow for 550 bed closures across the Board's area.

74 Tayside Health Board and its partners in Angus have viewed the approach to, and production of, the Mental Health strategy as a model for joint planned activities with other care groups, particularly for frail older people. Mr Young, Director of Commissioning and Strategic Management with the Health Board, said that his twin aims were to keep people on board with the strategy and to develop proposals that were sustained by all parties to the changes. He acknowledged that specific agreements about transferring resources from the Health Board to local authorities had been slow to emerge. He also acknowledged that an application for Bridging Finance to the Scottish Office from the Board has taken time to prepare but considered that it was important for all the parties to the planning to be assured of both their respective roles and their commitments.

75 New joint planning arrangements have been agreed between Angus Council and its main planning partners to take forward the development of the Community Care Plan for 1997-2000. The 3-tier structure includes representation at each tier from Tayside Health Board (which has delegated planning responsibilities to identified staff in a geographical basis reflecting the new unitary authority boundaries), Scottish Homes, the Housing

Department and the Social Work Department. In addition, the group with responsibility for developing the Plan in the first instance also includes representation from the local Healthcare Trust, GPs, the private and voluntary sectors, and from users' and carers' representatives. We were advised that the senior social work finance officer will be a member of the key planning group.

Purchasing

76 Angus Council does not have a written policy in relation to the purchase of services from the independent sector. In practice residential care is purchased from the private and voluntary sector; day care and some elements of home care are purchased from the voluntary sector. The Director of Social Work stated that the priority of Angus Council is to develop services which meet identified needs, within a mixed economy of care. He indicated that commissioning activity will increasingly be undertaken jointly with health and housing partners, particularly primary care services.

77 Angus Council is currently reviewing provision of home care service with a Value for Money (VFM) study aimed at the home help service. The VFM study is exploring two possible innovative developments. First, it is exploring a partnership with a voluntary agency that is in receipt of a substantial bequest; the partnership would be aimed at developing a befriending, shopping and pension-collection service. Secondly it is considering the development of community businesses in each of the localities, which would respond to the demand for support with domestic or household tasks. The outcome of this study is unknown at the time of writing.

IMPACT OF REGULATION AND CHARGING

Registration and inspection

78 On reorganisation, Angus Council established its own inspection and registration unit. It has a statutory responsibility to register and inspect independent sector residential and day care establishments for children and adults and for inspecting all establishments, including those of Angus Council. The Council has adopted the standards developed by the former Tayside Regional Council but these standards are now being reviewed. We were advised by Angus Council that negotiations are currently taking place with Tayside Health Board regarding the future joint working on inspection and the possibility of joint inspection standards.

Charging for non-residential services

79 It is not surprising that the introduction of charges generated a level of interest and, in some quarters, concern, amongst the local community and media. We were told that the council had introduced charges reluctantly, as a means of reducing the financial shortfall facing the new authority. Liability for charges is calculated on the basis of income, and services are provided free to individuals with an assessable income of less than £90 per week and to couples with an assessable income of less than £130 per week.

80 Prior to the introduction of charges, Angus Council issued information about the policy to all existing services users, and offered users the opportunity to complete a welfare benefits check, to establish whether they were eligible for any additional benefits. A report to the Social Work Committee on 28 May 1996 indicated that as a result of the benefits checks an additional £600,000 of benefits entitlement had been secured for people using non-residential care services.

81 The introduction of charges was not without difficulties, not least because of the scale of the exercise. Over 3000 people were initially identified as being in receipt of a service for which charges were to be introduced, and were accordingly sent information and subsequently visited. Technical hitches meant that there were delays in issuing the first bills, which were not sent out until July, although the intention is to bill users monthly in arrears. Because of these difficulties the council took the decision to waive all charges for April, but despite this, users had in fact received services for 2 months before receiving their first bill.

82 The original information leaflets appear to have been less helpful than expected, and were rapidly revised in the light of experience and comment. The revised leaflet does not advise service users that they may make "representations" against their assessed liability for charges, but does provide a contact point for anyone who thinks their bill is wrong. Some people have already made representations against their assessed liability for charges, and in a number of cases the Director of Social Work has exercised his power to reduce or waive charges where special circumstances are identified.

83 We understand that the Council will monitor the impact of the charging policy through quarterly reports which will identify the amount of income generated for the authority, the costs of collecting this, and the amount of additional benefit uptake as a result of the benefits checks. We were also advised that people who decline services on cost grounds will be contacted to assess the level of risk associated with this decision.

THE VIEWS OF SERVICE USERS IN ANGUS

84 We were interested in the views of residential and nursing home residents and of people in their own homes who used domiciliary care services, about the amount of information and choices they had been given when choosing these forms of care. In Angus we spoke to 26 service users, and received information from 2 carers: 15 people were in residential care, 2 were in nursing homes and 9 were receiving domiciliary services in their own homes. We received 2 questionnaires from carers; one was the carer of a person in a residential home, the other was the carer of a person in a nursing home.

Residential Care

85 The reasons for people's admission to residential care were split almost evenly between health problems and inability to cope in their own homes. None of the residents in the sample had considered other ways of meeting their needs, but a carer indicated that domiciliary care had been considered as another option. None reported having first heard of their home from any professional source, "family", "friends" or "its local reputation" being most frequently cited. None of the sample recalled being offered information to help them with the process of deciding on a home.

86 Half the sample (8 people) said that they had been offered a choice of home, whilst another 4 people indicated that they had made their decision about which home they wanted at an earlier stage. Most people (11) had received written information about the charges, and in one case the person's carer had also been given this information. There was no apparent difference in practice across the 3 sectors. Two private sector residents and the carer of a third had been told about the "topping up" arrangements if the chosen home cost more than the local authority would pay. One voluntary sector resident had been given this information. Two of the local authority residents said they had not been told about this, whilst the third was unsure. Two-thirds (6) of the private sector residents had initially been self-funding and 4 continued to be so. All of the voluntary sector residents were either fully or partially self-funding, as were 2 of the 3 local authority residents. Over half the sample (9 people) considered charges to be a "very important" factor influencing their decision about choice of home, whilst 2 more considered this to be "important".

Nursing Homes

87 There were 3 nursing home residents in this sample, including one whose carer completed a questionnaire. All were resident in private sector homes, had moved into care for health reasons or because they could no longer cope at home. None had considered other ways of meeting their needs.

88 One person had heard of the home from hospital staff, but none was given information to assist them in the process of finding an appropriate home.

89 All 3 respondents indicated that the decision about choice of home had already been made when they spoke with the social worker, and all received either written or verbal information about charges. Only one nursing home resident had been told about the possibility of "topping up" nursing home fees. One resident considered charges a "very important factor" influencing choice, whilst the carer who responded stated that they had been an "important" factor.

Domiciliary Services

90 Nine domiciliary service users who were receiving more than 10 hours of home help a week, were interviewed in Angus. Over half of them (5) had heard about services from hospital or community medical staff. Only 2 had learnt of services from social work staff. All were receiving between 2 services (in one case) and 6 services (in 3 cases). Only 3 older people had been offered a choice of services, and none had been offered a choice of agencies to provide those services.

91 Most (8) were receiving a home help service from the local authority (for which 2 people paid charges), whilst one person was paying for a private home help service. All those in the sample received chiropody services, and 8 received a community alarm. Other services mentioned were meals on wheels (5 users), Crossroads Care Attendant Scheme (2 users) and day care (one user).

92 Six users were paying for services, of whom 4 said they had received written information about charges. Four of the users who paid for services said that charges were an important factor influencing their decision about accepting services.

ANGUS

93 None of those interviewed had considered residential or nursing home care, although one person said that she would consider such a move in the future.

94 In addition to interviewing the 9 domiciliary service users in Angus, one self-completion questionnaire was also sent to the family carer of a tenth older person using domiciliary services, who had memory problems. This carer did not live with the older person. According to the carer, the service user was receiving 5 different community care services; home help, community nursing, residential respite, a sheltered housing alarm service and a tuck-in service.

95 This carer explained that deteriorating physical and mental health, together with the family's inability to cope, had led to the elderly person needing more help to manage at home. The carer was aware of a social worker / care manager visiting the service user to discuss her needs but did not know if the older person had received a copy of the written needs assessment or any information about what she had been assessed as needing by way of care. The carer had not been involved in discussing her relative's needs with social work.

96 The older person had received written information from the Council about service charges and considered these charges 'important' when deciding which services to accept. The importance of the cost of services to this family was highlighted by the carer indicating that although residential or nursing home care had not been suggested to the carer or the older person as a way of meeting their needs, the likely charges for this type of care would be reason for refusing to consider it.

Chapter 3

Dundee City Council

1. Dundee, one of Scotland's four major cities, is experiencing a decline in its overall population. In 1992 the population was 153,000. In 2006 it is estimated Dundee will have 140,000 residents. The new Dundee Council considered that the financial resources available to it were up to 8.4% less than had been available to its predecessors to meet similar needs. This was because the former Tayside Regional Council had directed a greater proportion of resources to urban Dundee, rather than to the other parts of Tayside and because the new Dundee Council boundaries were smaller than those of the old Dundee District.

2. Within the Social Work Department there are two principal managers for community care services, one for older people and one for adults with mental health problems, physical disability and learning disability. With the exception of home care (which is subject to review) services are divided between staff who assess and purchase community care services and those who provide them. The assessment and purchasing work is grouped under cost centre managers who operate in 3 geographical sectors of the City.

3. Dundee City Council makes available a wide range of care services to each of the community care groups: residential and nursing home care, domiciliary, day and respite care services are either provided directly by the Council or are purchased from the private and voluntary sectors. A specialist day care project for people with dementia is provided by Alzheimer's Scotland. There is a specialist centre, provided by the local authority, the Mackinnon Centre, which offers respite care and skills training to people with physical disabilities in all 3 authorities in the former Tayside Region. The White Top Centre, managed by the local authority, provides day care for adults with profound learning disabilities, and also offers 3 respite care places to all 3 authorities. Residential care for those with substance misuse problems is provided by the voluntary sector, whilst The Wishart Centre offers day care services to this group. Specialist help for people with HIV or AIDS is largely provided by Dundee as lead authority in partnership with the voluntary sector. Headway, a voluntary organisation, provides specialist support to people who have suffered head injuries. The voluntary sector is a major partner of the local authority in the provision of community care services in Dundee City.

4. The Community Care Action Plan for Dundee estimates that within the area there are:

3,759 adults (age 16-64) with a severe or very severe physical disability;

475 adults with learning disabilities, of whom 87 have profound disability;

3,700 adults with a severe mental illness;

2,400 adults at high risk of alcohol dependency;

600 adults who are injecting drugs.

5. The Plan does not provide an estimate of the number of people within the authority who are HIV positive or who have AIDS.

Needs and provision for older people

6. Dundee City's Community Care Action Plan uses figures from the Mid-Year Population Estimates provided by the General Register Office (Scotland) to calculate that in 1994 there were 9983 people over the age of 75. Estimates from the same source indicate that the number of older people over 85 has increased to over 2,400 persons, compared to 2261 in 1990.

7. Using these data, and employing the Intervals of Need model developed by Isaacs,[16] we estimated that of all older people aged 75 and above in Dundee:

between 2,250 and 3,350 require intensive levels of support;

between 400 and 1,100 require regular support more than once each day;

between 1,900 and 2,700 require help solely with domestic tasks.

8. The difference between the smaller and larger numbers depends on the amount of support older people obtain from their family, or other carers. If no families in Dundee were prepared or able to support those older people who require intensive levels of support, 3,350 older people would have to obtain their support from public agencies.

Existing provision of community care services for older people

9. Older people requiring intensive support may obtain their support in either residential or community settings. Using the above figures based on Isaacs' model, and statistical information routinely provided to, or available to The Scottish Office, we estimated that for older people requiring intensive levels of support in Dundee, in 1995/96:

a total of 218 "units of support"[17] were available, per 1000 people aged over 75 years;

less than a quarter of the available provision was within hospital (48 places per 1000 people aged 75+);

residential and nursing homes provided more than double the available hospital provision 150 places per 1000 people aged 75+);

there was relatively little intensive support for people at home, although some older people's needs were met, in part, through a high level of provision of sheltered housing (21 people per 1000 people aged 75+ received a home help service 6 or 7 days per week).

10. These figures suggest that in Dundee, community care services for older people who need intensive support, are mainly focused on the residential and nursing home sectors. There are few social care officers, or home help staff providing the intensive support older people and their families may require.

11. The same data suggest that some older people with a need for regular support during the day may also experience difficulty in obtaining a range of appropriate support. Whilst

day care provision is around the national average, the home help service is provided to less than half this group on more than 2 days a week. In contrast, the widespread availability of sheltered housing, community alarms and aids to daily living indicate that packages of care for people who need regular support can sustain these older people in their own homes, when linked to nursing services.

12. On the basis of these estimates, it seems that the people who are best served by existing community care services are those older people who require assistance solely with domestic tasks. The home help service has been able to provide relatively short periods of support for those who need assistance with household tasks, shopping and the collection of pensions.

Residential and nursing home care

13. Table 7 below shows the places in residential and nursing homes when Dundee City Council took over responsibility on 1st April 1996.

	No of Beds	Percent of Total	Occupancy (%)	Scotland (%)
Residential Homes				
Local Authority	401	27%	95	91
Private	162	11%	83	88
Voluntary	163	11%	95	92
Nursing Homes	770	51%	66	85
Total	1496	100%		

Table 7: Residential and Nursing Home Beds in Dundee City on 1st April 1996.

14 Local Authority residential home beds comprised 27% of the available bed spaces within the Dundee area on 31 March 1996. On 1st July 1996 Dundee closed Strathmore House, one of its own homes, with 36 bed spaces. There has been a decline in local authority beds for older people across Scotland during the last 10 years. Across all providers (local authority, private and voluntary sectors) the number of residential beds has recently shown a decrease, due in large part to conversion to single rooms in existing homes.

15 In contrast to residential homes, bed spaces in Scottish nursing homes have almost quadrupled in the last decade. Dundee has reflected this trend. At June 1996 the overall number of nursing home beds in Dundee was 826.

16 Currently in Dundee, occupancy rates (that is the number of residents compared to the number of beds) are higher in local authority homes than in private sector homes. Occupancy rates in nursing homes are continuing to fall, because although admission rates have increased, the number of beds has increased at a faster rate.

17 Since 1 April, 1996 Dundee City Council has been purchasing residential care in private and voluntary sector homes as well as placing people in its own homes. Table 8 below shows the most recent pattern of admission to residential and nursing home care.

	No of Admissions	Percent of Total
Residential Homes		
Local Authority	27	33%
Private	8	10%
Voluntary	5	6%
Nursing Homes	41	51%
Total	81	100%

Table 8: Admissions to Residential and Nursing Home Care in Dundee City
1.4.96 – 18.7.96

18 The use made of private sector residential and nursing homes by Dundee City Council has been the subject of complaint by private sector providers who claim the local authority place people in local authority homes more readily. Two thirds of all admissions in the period studied were to the independent sector and one third to local authority homes. The relative admission rates match the relative distribution of beds.

Day care

19 Dundee City Council operates two day care establishments for older people, Wellgate and Menzieshill.

20 The 2 day centres are open 7 days a week providing meals, leisure activities and personal care. At Menzieshill an average of 15 users attend the day centre during the week, and as many as 13 on Saturday and Sunday. At Wellgate average attendance is over 40 during the week, and 20 at weekends.

21 Dundee City Council also spot purchases some day care, and gives grants to a few voluntary community care organisations who provide day care support. Their contribution is not quantified here.

Home care

22 In May 1996 the home help service in Dundee City remained a service provided to many older people but for few hours. Over 85% of older people using home helps received the service for 3 hours or less each week. The service was oriented mainly towards providing domestic support rather than personal care. Less than 16% of users received personal care. Dundee has since informed us that personal care is most often delivered by the voluntary sector at present and that the Council sees this partnership as growing strongly in the future.

23 From information available to us the provision of meals, both mobile and at lunch clubs appears to be above the Scottish average, as do the number of community alarms. Occupational therapy support – through the provision of aids to daily living, and advice on adaptations – is at the Scottish average. The introduction of social care officers is an important contribution to providing intensive care at home.

24 Dundee City Council is the main provider of sheltered housing in Dundee. With other providers of sheltered housing (including medium dependency housing) Dundee Council has provision for 46% of the population over 75. This range of housing, supported in large part by a warden service, contributes substantially to the capacity of the City Council to provide care at home.

The Quality of Care in Residential and Nursing Homes in Dundee City

25 We examined quality on the basis of the reports available on the most recent annual inspection in 22 homes in Dundee; the sample comprised 7 private homes, 6 of the 7 voluntary homes and 9 local authority homes.[18] Eighteen of these reports relate to inspections carried out by the inspection unit of Tayside Regional Council. Four reports, one each on a voluntary and on a private sector home, and 2 on local authority homes, were compiled by the new inspection unit of Dundee City Council since 1 April 1996. We understand that the new authority plans to review the existing standards.

26 We also examined the reports prepared by Tayside Health Board in relation to three nursing homes in Dundee.

27 Across all sectors, the highest average number of standards met was in respect of standards relating to "accommodation and facility", whilst the lowest was in relation to "medication". The local authority scored the lowest in relation to staffing standards, where the average percentage of standards met was 90%, compared with 93% by the private sector and 95% by the voluntary sector. Figure 4 below, shows the average percentage of standards met by residential homes across the sectors. These percentages were calculated by taking the number of standards met as a proportion of the total number applied in each section of every inspection report and dividing the total by the number of homes in each sector. The total average was calculated by adding the number of standards met by the homes in each sector and expressing this as a percentage of the total number of standards.

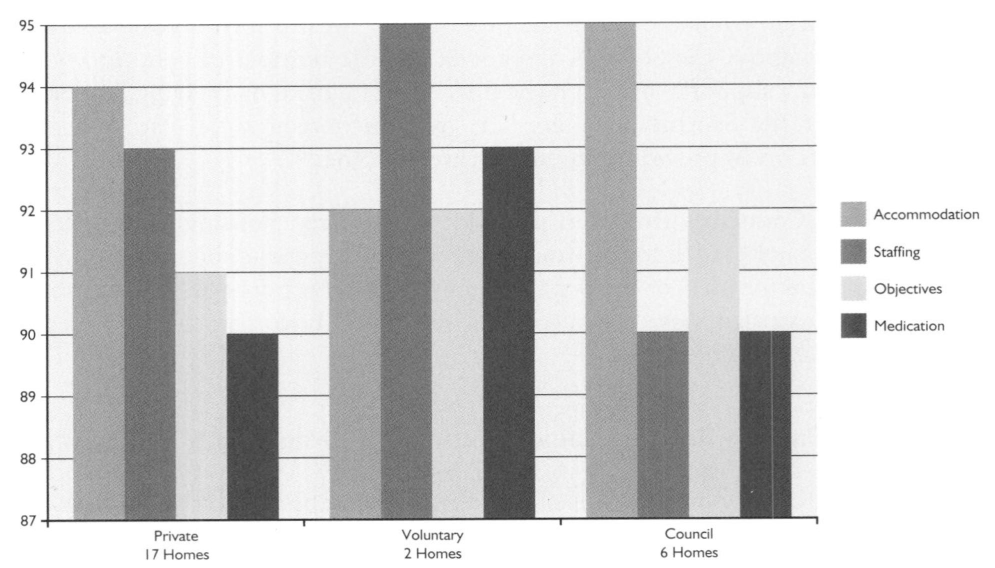

Figure 4: Average Percentage of Standards Met in Residential Homes by Sector in Dundee City.

28 Being able to make choices is as important to older people in homes as it is to everyone else. One very important choice is that of being able to choose not to share a bedroom with someone else. Figure 5 below shows that the Council homes offer significantly more choice in this regard. For all sectors the proportion of beds available as single rooms is high and reflects increasingly higher overall standards of provision in residential care.

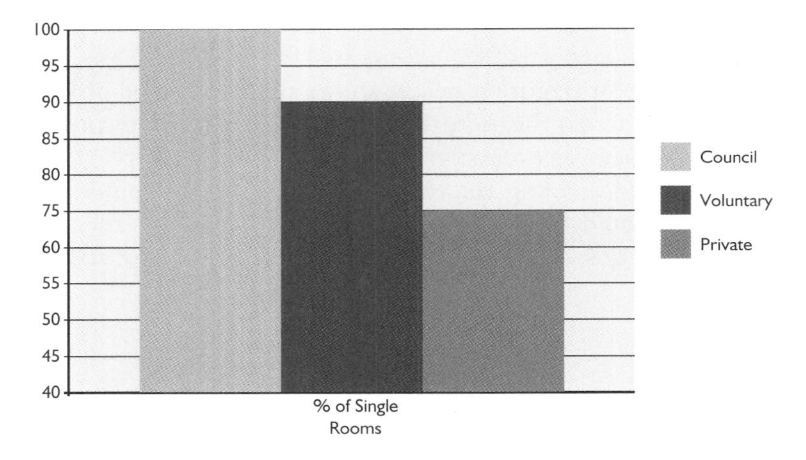

Figure 5: Percentage of Beds Available in Single Rooms By Sector in Dundee City.

29 Choices about planning your care and about menus and food are also important. We undertook a more detailed analysis on a sub-set of standards regarding the availability of these choices. We analysed the reports to compare the standards regarding older people's involvement in the construction of their care plans, whether their individual likes and dislikes about food were taken into account by homes and whether they were involved in or consulted about menu planning. Table 9 below shows the number of homes which met the standards across the sectors.

Standard	Local Authority	Private	Voluntary
Care Plan involvement 2.28,2.31,2.32,2.35 or 2.36	Met in 7 out of 9 homes.	Met in 5 out of 7 homes.	Met in 5 out of 6 homes.
Menu Planning Involvement 2.60, 2.63,2.66,2.67,2.70, 2.71or 2.72.	Met in 7 out of 9 homes.	Met in 6 out of 7 homes.	Met in all 6 homes.
Individual food preferences met 2.61,2.64,2.67,2.68, 2.71 2.72 or 2.73	Met in all 9 homes.	Met in all 7 homes.	Met in all 6 homes.

Note: The numbering given to the same standards varied between individual inspection reports, both within and across authorities. This is indicated at Column 1 of the Table.

Table 9: Proportion of Homes in Each Sector Meeting Selected Standards on Choices in Dundee City.

30 The standards which were not met in the independent sector homes related to the absence of written policies or procedures, and to lack of evidence that residents were aware of their care plans, had been actively involved in their construction and had signed them. Other shortfalls related to records of individual residents' personal possessions and written policies and records concerning the administration of medication. Some homes had inadequate procedures for admission and discharge of residents. The overall impression was that the quality of care was satisfactory but that structural improvements were required in some homes, such as the provision of an adapted toilet for use by residents with disabilities. The inspection unit had given homes three years in which to carry out these major structural improvements in recognition of the capital expenditure involved.

31 The overall average number of standards met by homes in Dundee is high in all sectors. Staffing ratios were not at the inspection and registration standard in all homes in any sector. The proportion of single bedrooms in Dundee private sector homes is relatively low at 74% compared with 100% in local authority homes and 89% in voluntary homes.

Nursing Homes

32 Our conclusions about quality in nursing homes are based on recent reports of inspections in three nursing homes in Dundee. Quality of care in the three nursing homes inspected in Dundee was found by Health Board inspectors to be generally good. However, shortfalls in aspects of the medication procedures were highlighted in all three homes and care plans in two of the three homes were also said to require attention. A number of minor refurbishments such as providing bathroom towel rails and installing safety guards for heaters were also recommended. In one home there were concerns that the regime was unduly restrictive, since residents could only go into the garden with the permission of staff. Only one of the three homes had inadequate staffing levels but this same home had recorded 122 minor accidents in the preceding 12 months, mostly consisting of falls, cuts and bruises. Occupancy levels in the three homes were variable; two homes reported levels of 43% and 45% respectively, while the third home had almost three quarters (74%) of its beds occupied.

33 At present Tayside Health Board does not make Nursing Home inspection reports available to the local authority.

The Frailty of Older People living in Residential and Nursing Homes in Dundee City

34 We compared frailty levels in 2 distinct kinds of provision, residential homes and nursing homes, as well as between sectors. We used information about frailty in residential homes, which is routinely submitted to The Scottish Office on an annual basis. We examined these data in relation to all local authority homes and a random, but broadly representative sample of homes run by private and voluntary organisations. Finally we examined nursing home inspection reports provided to us by Tayside Health Board.

35 Our sample in Dundee comprised 9 local authority residential homes, 4 private and 3 voluntary residential homes, and 3 nursing homes.

36 We looked at 3 types of frailty: incontinence; people who are bed or chair-bound; people who are "confused". The definition of "confusion" adopted by Social Work Services Group when requesting statistical returns from local authorities refers to people "whose mental confusion arises from brain pathology and is of permanent and irreversible nature, and who require regular supervision or help to perform tasks of daily living, or constant care because of aimless wandering etc." The definition of confusion used by medical staff when someone is admitted to a nursing home, or by a visiting member of an inspection team may be different.

37 One nursing home has a significantly higher percentage of "confused" residents (92%) than the others, but incontinence levels are broadly similar, ranging from 54% – 61%. In one nursing home no residents are described as chair or bedbound, and only 4% are so described in the other 2 homes in our sample.

38 Levels of incontinence in local authority homes are generally low, and only in 3 homes does the level rise above 25%. Levels of "confusion" range from less than 10% in one home to nearly half the residents in two other homes (46% and 47%). Only a small percentage of residents in local authority homes and in nursing homes are said to be either chair or bedbound.

39 The private homes in Dundee are catering for a mixture of frailties among older people. One home does not have any of its residents described as "confused", incontinent or chair or bedbound. A second home does not have any "confused" or incontinent residents, but has 5% who are chair or bedbound. Levels of confusion are lower than in all but one of the local authority homes in Dundee, whilst levels of incontinence are similar.

40 The sample of 3 voluntary sector homes in Dundee includes 2 homes with a higher proportion of chair or bedbound residents than in either the private or local authority sectors. The home with the highest proportion of chair or bedbound residents (36%), also has the highest proportion of people who are incontinent (56%). Only one home has over a fifth of its residents described as "confused" (23%), which is similar to one of the private homes (21%) and towards the lower end of the range of "confusion" in local authority homes.

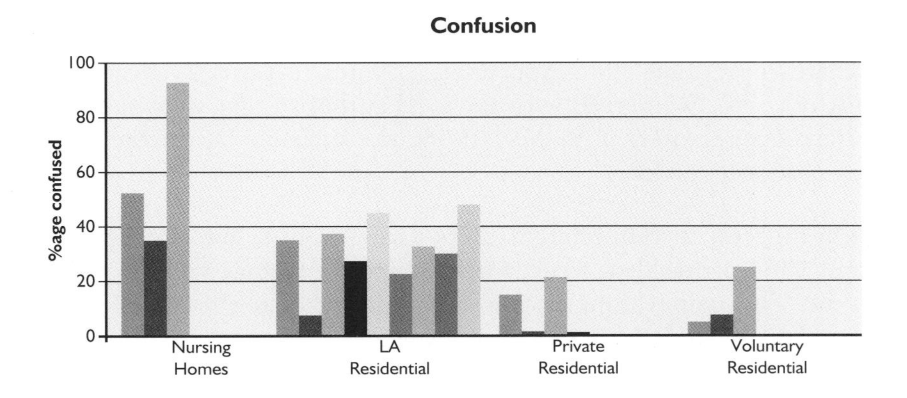

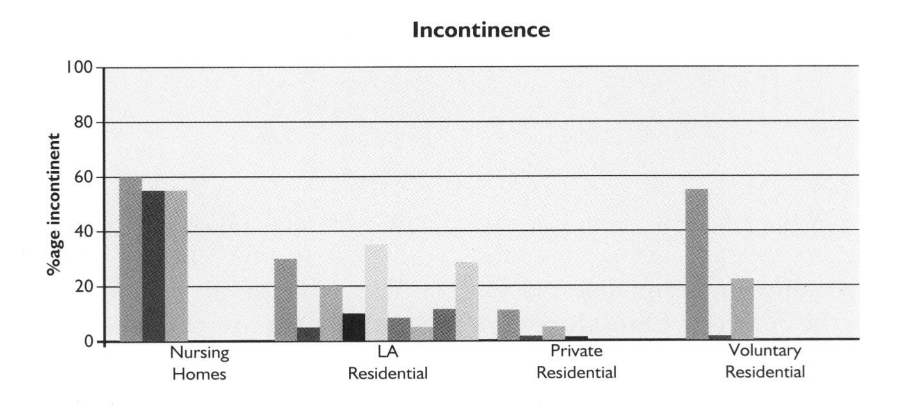

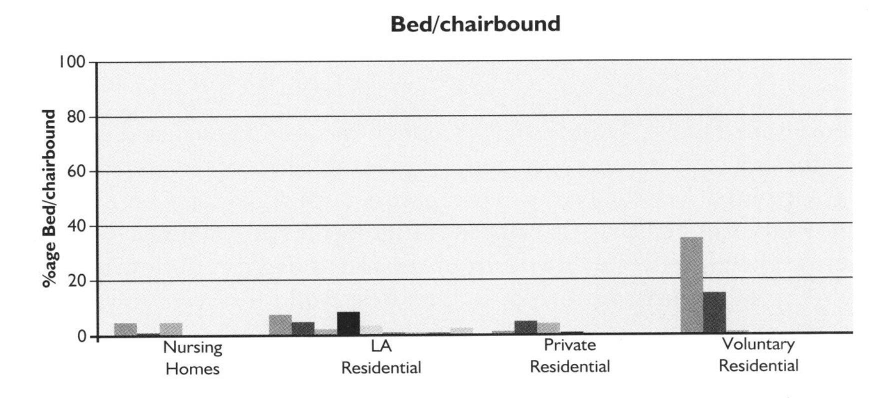

Figure 6: Frailty Levels in Residential and Nursing Homes in Dundee.

COSTS OF COMMUNITY CARE SERVICES

Local Authority Residential Care

41 Currently, within the Council, there are nine residential units : Menzieshill House which provides both residential and day care; and Ancrum House, Craigie House, Douglas House, Harefield House, Janet Brougham House, Marryat House, St Leonard's House and Turriff House which all provide residential care only.

42 We calculated the actual costs of each of these homes, using figures supplied by the Councils themselves, and applying the current costing formula and guidance issued by COSLA and CIPFA, where appropriate. (See Appendix 2, Notes to Costs Analysis and Appendix 3 for a full list of costs). We agreed with the local authority that we would use the number of long-term residents (363) at 31 May 1996, as a snapshot, to enable us to calculate average weekly costs per resident.

43 The average weekly full cost in the different units varied from a low of £291 per resident week to a high of £364 per resident week, with a weighted average weekly cost of £313 per resident per week. The main reasons for this divergence relate to the capital value of the buildings and numbers of beds (and therefore levels of occupancy) in individual homes. The average number of residents in the two most expensive homes are 28 and 31 residents respectively compared to an average of 43 residents in the others. Since many costs are fixed in nature, lower bed numbers can increase unit costs. There was no significant difference in the weighted average costs of the other homes, which were around £304 per week.

Domiciliary Care

44 The average cost per hour for the provision of domiciliary care in Dundee is £6.16. Most of these costs relate to staff, and account for approximately 96% of care costs. However, with no overhead costs being allocated to domiciliary care by the Council the calculated cost is below the 'full cost'. Our calculations suggest that the cost of domiciliary care is less than the £6.50 cost published by the Council in its Community Care Action Plan, although we recognise that the Plan's costings are based on figures for the former Tayside Regional Council.

Day Care

45 In addition to Menzieshill House, Dundee City Council has one specialist day care unit, Wellgate. The cost for day care at the 2 local authority establishments averaged £35 and £40 per day, with a weighted weekly average cost, across both units, of £36.11. We were informed by Dundee City Council that the snapshot user figures at 31 May 1996, on which these calculations are based, reflect a downturn in the use of day care following the introduction of charges. Any subsequent upturn in usage rates would lead to a reduction in the average weekly cost per person.

46 The weighted average full cost of day care is £36 per day, considerably higher than the £22 cost published in the Community Action Care Plan.

Performance against Standard Rate

47 Section 22 of the National Assistance Act 1948 requires local authorities to set a standard rate for local authority residential care within their area; this amount should equate to the actual average cost of its own homes.

	Standard Rate	Average Cost Calculated
Residential Care	£320/week	£313/week

The Council's average full cost is below the published standard rate for residential care.

Comparative Costs and Potential Savings

48 Currently, within Dundee, independent sector providers are paid between £203 and £244 per week for residential care, depending on the care needs catered for and the facilities provided. The figure of £216.88, used in the Table below, is the average cost paid to the independent sector by the local authority, taking account of these premiums. The original figures were supplied by the Council.

49 Eligible residents placed in the independent sector receive from the Department of Social Security a Residential Allowance of £54.00 per week; this £54.00 is remitted to the local authority. No similar allowance is received by individuals placed in a local authority home. In addition, dependent on which sector the resident is in, a different level of income support is available. We have not included Attendance Allowances payable in the first four weeks, due to their marginal impact on costing.

50 Table 10 below shows the costs to Dundee City Council of placing a resident in an independent sector home compared with the average costs of maintaining places in their own homes.

	Local Authority £	Independent £
Gross average cost per resident to local authority/price paid per resident by local authority	312.78	216.88
Less : Income received by local authority		
Residential Allowance	–	(54.00)
Income Support Premiums (Note 1[19])	–	(23.23)
Income Support (Note 2[20])	(48.00)	(34.15)
Net cost to local authority	264.78	105.50

Table 10: Comparative Costs to Dundee City Council of Local Authority Provision and Purchase from Independent Sector of Residential Care.

51 Table 10 shows that Dundee City Council could make savings by placing more residents in the independent sector. To identify the scale of the potential gross savings available to the local authority it is first necessary to consider costs that would not be saved. These fall into three areas.

52 First, some overhead costs and a proportion of the cost of capital would not be saved.

53 Secondly, the costs of effecting the closure of homes would need to be taken into account. Closure of local authority homes would either require redeployment of staff within the authority, or redundancies, or transfer to new providers. Each of these options would to some extent limit the savings which could be made. If homes were sold to private or voluntary sector providers the new owners might take on existing staff from the homes.

These staff would, of course, be covered by the application of the Transfer of Undertakings (Protection of Employment) Regulations 1981, and it is possible, indeed likely, that new owners would be reluctant to accept such transfers.

54 The cost in the early years of closing or transfering homes to the independent sector might very substantially reduce the savings realised, particularly if redundancy costs all fell in the first year. In addition, and depending on the arrangements made, local authorities might not benefit from the £54 DSS income until the new provision had been established for some years.

55 Thirdly, a number of factors might contribute to rises in the price of places in the independent sector and thus further reduce the potential savings. To bring all the independent sector provision up to the standard of the Council's own provision in respect of single room accommodation would be likely to lead to price increases. Moreover it is arguable that the price charged to the Council by private and voluntary homes is artificially low and can only be sustained by higher charges made for privately financed placements and by some 'hidden costs' of services charged for particular services provided to individual residents. If the proportion of privately and publicly financed placements changed then arguably the charge to the Council could rise. Independent sector bodies have argued strongly that the prices paid by the Council are not sufficient.

56 It is not possible to quantify the effects of these diverse elements and a reasonable judgement must be made. It would be unrealistic for the Council to envisage that it could make savings proportionate to the variation in weekly cost given in Table 10. Nevertheless we consider that the Council could make more cost-effective use of its resources by making significantly greater use of independent sector provision and that realistically the potential savings could be between £1.3 million and £2.6 million which could be otherwise applied to enhance community care services[21].

57 These considerations point to ensuring that a realistic view is taken of potential savings and careful management of any changes. Managing any substantial change in services for vulnerable people requires great care on the part of the local authority and may only be achieved successfully over a period of time. The authority must plan its change strategy well, must allow sufficient time for implementation, and must communicate its intentions to service users and carers, to their own staff and to the wider public, in a way which is both informative and reassuring about the continuing care which will be available. This requires local authorities to make a realistic appraisal of the most cost-efficient mixed economy for their area, and to plan a strategy to achieve this within a realistic timescale.

Budget Setting and Control

58 Our review of Dundee Council's budgetary control mechanisms for 1996/97 identified that budgets had been incrementally set using as the base year a disaggregated Tayside Regional budget. Whilst the Council would like to develop a needs led approach to setting the 1997/98 budget, budget options are limited as there is a commitment to fixed staff costs of approximately 80% of budget. The budget is currently being prepared with input from both Corporate Finance who calculate the "bottom line" budget; and social work finance who prepare a more detailed budget taking into account this base. The

Director of Social Work is then subject to extensive questioning by the Council leader, Chairman, Chief Executive, Director of Finance and Director of Personnel to ensure that no "extras" have been built in to the budget.

59 Budgets within the Social Work Department can be devolved below the level of cost centres. Unit managers, home care managers, senior social workers and care managers can all be budget holders. In general, budgets are devolved to the level at which resources are committed. For the purchase of independent sector care, the budget is managed by the managers for older people's services and adult care, in conjunction with the Manager (Finance, I.T. and Human Resources). Some arrangement of this kind is necessary if limited budgets are to be managed effectively. As new arrangements are brought in we would expect the Council to take forward plans for greater budgetary devolution.

60 Monitoring is carried out through regular meetings with budget holders, through the provision of financial information and through financial analyses conducted by finance staff from the social work department and the finance department. Budget holders also maintain their own systems for monitoring expenditure in critical areas, e.g. a spreadsheet is updated weekly to show commitments against the residential and nursing home budget.

61 The authority is continuing to work to develop further budget monitoring and control procedures, and is providing financial training to assist budget holders to manage their budgets effectively. We were informed that the continued development of the K2 computerised client database system will eventually lead to the alignment of current financial and management information system. We understand, however, that this is unlikely to occur within the next four to five years.

PLANNING AND PURCHASING

62 The revised Community Care Action Plan (1996/97) for Dundee City Council is a revised and updated version of the Community Care Action Plan originally prepared by the former Tayside Regional Council with Tayside Health Board. Information contained in the earlier document was disaggregated to the level of the new unitary authorities. The introduction to the Plan summarises how the new authority proposes to take forward objectives previously deferred and notes that at that time the authors "were not in a position to draw up a definitive statement of intended actions".

63 The current Action Plan provides a set of broad brush statements about planned actions by Social Work and other agencies to achieve a series of key objectives in relation to each of the community care groups. Where applicable the funding source for these proposals is clearly stated. The Plan also provides information about the nature and scope of the consultations on the draft, and provides statistical data and estimates of need.

64 However, the Plan is generally lacking in detail. It does not provide information about intended levels of service over the planning period, nor does it provide measurable objectives and targets for service providers. General statements such as "Improve flexibility and range of home care support...", or "Continue expansion of Home from Home respite care by advertising, recruiting and training volunteers" are used rather than the more specific and measurable "Improve flexibility ... by [specific action]" or "Continue expansion ... by recruiting and training [number] of volunteers".

65 The Plan provides a range of statistical data in relation to each community care service area, but makes little attempt to relate assessed aggregate needs to current services, with a view to identifying service shortfalls. The Plan also lacks information about the financial resources and assumptions underpinning the planned actions, and does not provide either clear outputs or outcomes in relation to these intentions. Finally, the Plan does not provide a clear statement of the authority's purchasing intentions, although it does give information about the pattern of purchasing by Tayside Regional Council in the preceding year. We have been told by Dundee that the new Community Care Plan for 1997-2000, will, as far as possible, contain sufficient detailed information to permit its use as a management tool.

66 Joint planning with Tayside Health Board has continued outwith the Community Care Plan. Dundee City Council, alongside Angus and Perth & Kinross Councils have agreed much of the framework for the transfer of resources between the Health Board and individual local authorities. Dundee has been a partner in the work to disaggregate the 1996/97 tranche of Resource Transfer of £2.3m, Tayside Health Board anticipates that £19m will be transferred to the three authorities during the current 4-year programme. This will allow for 550 bed closures across the Board's area. In 1996/97 Dundee will receive £1,680,000 a small part of which (£180,000) is related to programme of continuing care bed closures at King's Cross hospital.

67 The Director of Social Work, Mr Bates, stated that working relationships between Tayside Health Board and Dundee City Council were good. He considered that the arrangements for Resource Transfer took into account both the tensions that the health service faced and the importance of enabling all parties to work together. He stressed the importance of changes having support within the community in which the changes would take place. He spoke of the arrangements for joint assessment, hospital discharge, the development of a pricing structure for Resource Transfer and the implementation of the Continuing Care Circular as being evidence of the sound partnership with the Health Board.

68 Revised planning arrangements have been set in place between the authority and its planning partners, and the process of developing the new Plan has commenced. Dundee City Council and its partners have adopted a relatively streamlined, 2-tier planning structure, which includes the active involvement of the senior finance officer from the Social Work Department.

Purchasing

69 The Director of Social Work stressed that Dundee City Council was reviewing its policies about the purchase of care. He emphasised that Dundee City Council was a different body to the former Tayside Regional Council, drawing attention to the Council's Corporate Plan. The Plan, referring to partnerships with "any group or body which can make a positive contribution", states that "the Council believes that there is no significant objective which can be achieved without forming strong partnerships with others in the private, public or voluntary sectors."

70 Mr Bates emphasised in interview, and subsequently wrote to us stressing, the importance of the local authority continuing in its role as a provider of services within a

mixed economy of care. As a direct provider, he writes that: "Local Authorities can demonstrate an even handed approach to standards, competencies, outcomes and quality which can then generate regulations and standards for other providers." Mr Bates states that "the 'mixed economy of care' was...intended to ensure diversity, choice, stability and continuity for some of the most vulnerable citizens in our community, and to remove the direct provision of public services from this equation would put this objective greatly at risk."

71 A senior officer viewed the Direction on Choice as being the critical factor in determining placement decisions. She stated that people who were assessed as needing residential care tended to favour local authority provision; she said this reflected the prevailing culture of the city, namely a commitment to public services. This statement contrasts with one of the findings from the consultations on the draft Community Care Plan. In the plan there is a comment that "People who are not self-funding were unaware that they could choose a home run by the private sector."

72 The local authority continues to be the major provider of both day and domiciliary care, although private sector providers were said to have begun to show some interest in day care provision. Considerable use is already made of the voluntary sector to deliver the latter. There is no private sector involvement in domiciliary care. The local authority is also the main provider of respite care, although the former Tayside Regional Council went out to tender for these services. The response was disappointing – only 3 private sector providers submitted tenders, at prices which were not considered to be financially advantageous to the authority.

IMPACT OF REGULATION AND CHARGING

Registration and inspection

73 On reorganisation, Dundee City Council established its own inspection and registration unit. It is responsible for registering residential and day care establishments for children and adults in the independent sector and for inspecting all establishments, including those of Dundee City Council. The Council has adopted the standards developed by Tayside Regional Council.

74 Mr Bates said he was working towards establishing a joint inspection and registration unit with the Health Board by the end of the financial year 1996/97. We were told that the local authority considers this to be a development priority which would promote collaborative practice on inspections, and a sharing of resources. A longer term objective is to agree common standards in anticipation of the development of a "one care home" and a new regulatory framework.

Charging for non-residential services

75 Charges for home care services were introduced by Dundee City Council as a means of generating income to meet an identified financial shortfall. The charges are based on a calculation of the actual cost of each service, and on an assessment of each service user's income. Services are provided free to individuals with an income of less than £90 per week,

and to couples with an income of less than £125 per week. The council has undertaken to review the effects of this policy at the end of its first year.

76 We were told that the authority was concerned not to create disincentives against the use of services, and that the charges had been based on both a calculation of the likely level of income to be generated, and an estimate of what the local community would consider to be "reasonable".

77 All home care service users were advised of the intention to introduce charges personally and by letter, and were offered a welfare benefits check to ensure that they were in receipt of their full benefits entitlement. It was not clear whether users were advised that they could make representations against their assessed liability for charges

78 We were advised that the council would monitor the impact of its policy through an examination of all cases where existing services were cancelled by users and following these up by letter and personal contact. It was also expected that they would analyse service take-up/rejection rates by people newly assessed as requiring the service. Current calculations suggested that 71% of those paying charges were paying the full cost and the officer we spoke to did not think it would be feasible to follow up the remaining 29% who, presumably, are on lower income levels and might experience some hardship.

THE VIEWS OF SERVICE USERS IN DUNDEE

79 We sought the views of a sample of residential and nursing home residents, and users of domiciliary care services in their own homes and in very sheltered housing about the amount of information and choice they were given when deciding on these forms of care. We spoke to 27 service users in Dundee, and received questionnaires from 8 carers. Five people were in residential care, 3 were in nursing homes, 9 were in very sheltered housing and 10 were in receipt of domiciliary care in their own homes. We received one questionnaire from the carer of a person in a residential home, 4 from carers of people in nursing homes and 3 from carers of people using domiciliary services in their own homes.

Residential Care

80 The 5 people interviewed and the carer offered "health" or "not coping" as the reason for seeking admission to residential care. Only one person had considered other ways of meeting their needs, through domiciliary care services. One resident had heard about the Home from a social worker, and one from a doctor.

81 No data was available on whether 4 of the cases in the sample had been given information to help decide on a suitable home, but one person in local authority accommodation indicated that they had been given both written and verbal information.

82 The carer of the voluntary sector resident had been offered a choice of accommodation across all 3 sectors. Two local authority residents had not been offered a choice, and two were unsure of this. One of the local authority residents stated that he could not be given a choice because the offered home was the only one available, even though it was not in that individual's own home area.

83 The private sector resident stated that information about charges had not been offered. The carer of the voluntary sector resident, and one local authority resident both indicated that they had been given information verbally. Only the carer of the voluntary sector resident had been advised of the "topping up" arrangements. Charges were felt to have been a "very important" factor influencing the choice of the voluntary sector carer (who was partially self-financing) and of one local authority resident (who was funded by the local authority), but were "not at all important" in the other 4 cases.

Nursing Homes

84 Interviews were conducted with 3 nursing home residents, and questionnaires were completed by the carers of 4 more residents. All residents had sought admission to residential care for health reasons, and only one resident reported having considered meeting identified needs in other ways – in this case, by domiciliary care. Residents or carers learnt of the home(s) from medical staff in 2 cases, and from a social worker in one case. Only one resident said that they had been given information to help with the process of deciding on a home.

85 One resident was offered a choice of homes, whilst 2 said that they were not offered any choice. Three carers indicated that they had been offered choices. One carer and one resident had been given written information about charges, and another resident had been given verbal information. Two carers said that they had been given no information about charges. None of the carers had been told about "topping up" arrangements, although 2 residents had been told and the third was unsure about this point. Two residents were fully self-financing, whilst the third was partly self-financing. Two carers indicated that the people for whom they cared were partly self-financing. Three carers considered that charges had been either "important" or "very important" in affecting the decision on choice of a Home, whilst this was not seen as a significant factor by any of the residents who were interviewed.

Very Sheltered Housing

86 Nine tenants of very sheltered housing were interviewed in Dundee. Although most mentioned a number of reasons for this move, all but one mentioned health as being the main reason. Most (8) had heard of the facility from someone in the social work department – either from a social worker (6 cases), or, in one case each, from a home help organiser or a care manager.

87 Almost half the sample (4 cases) had considered either residential or nursing home care: two had tried nursing home care and did not like it, another had visited a residential home but had not liked it and had thought the charges too high. The remaining 5 tenants had not considered other ways of meeting their needs.

88 Six of the tenants had been receiving services to help them at home before they moved into very sheltered housing. Most (5) had been receiving home help, 2 had also received a meals service and one was also using Crossroads' services.

89 In addition to the services provided by the staff of the very sheltered housing, all of the tenants in the sample were receiving at least one community-based service. Most

tenants in the sample (7) received chiropody services. The next most frequently-mentioned service was the home help service: 4 tenants received this service from the local authority, whilst 2 were purchasing services privately, at a cost of approximately £5 per hour. Other tenants were receiving a variety of services, including Crossroads (2 cases), community nurse (2 cases) day hospital (2 cases) and psychiatric nurse (one case).

90 When asked whether there had been any changes to their services since 1 April 1996, 4 tenants mentioned the introduction of charges for the home help service, and the 2 who received private home helps explained that these were now cheaper than the local authority service. Three tenants said that they had received information about the introduction of charges. Six tenants were paying for the community services they received and 4 of these had received written information about the introduction of charges. Most (5) of those paying for services said that charges were not an important factor influencing their decision to accept these services, although one tenant said that they were an important factor.

91 Only three of the tenants who were interviewed had been offered a choice of services and providers.

Domiciliary Services

92 Ten domiciliary care users who were receiving 10 or more hours of home care, were interviewed in Dundee. Most had learnt about available services from social work or medical staff (4 in each case). All were receiving between 2 services (in 2 cases) and 8 services (one case). All were receiving a home help service, for which half were paying, and 6 received a chiropody service. The community alarm service, meals on wheels and hairdressing services were each also used by 4 people in this sample.

93 Half of those interviewed said that they had been offered a choice about the type of service which could be available to them, but most (8) said that they had not been offered a choice of provider.

94 Only one user was not paying for any of the services received. Four people said they had received written information about what the charges would be, and 4 had not. Two could not remember. Users were split about the importance of charges in coming to a decision about which services to use. Four people said that charges had been an important factor, whilst 5 said they had not been important.

95 Most (9) of those interviewed said that they had never considered moving into residential or nursing home care, but 2 people said they would consider it in the future, whilst one said her General Practitioner had already suggested it.

96 Three carers returned questionnaires about domiciliary care services. In each case the service user was receiving between three and ten services, and in 2 cases the service user and/or carer had been offered a choice of services and a choice, for some services, of local authority or voluntary provider. In 2 cases users were paying for services. In both cases they had received written information about charges and the charges were felt to have been important in determining which services were accepted. Residential or nursing home care had been considered in both these cases, and the carers indicated that costs would be a key factor in any future decision about these types of care.

Chapter 4

Perth & Kinross Council

1 Perth & Kinross Council is responsible for one of the largest rural areas in Scotland, with a population of 132,000. Perth is the largest conurbation and administrative centre. Kinross, Blairgowrie and Pitlochry are the other towns in an otherwise widely scattered population. The Social Work Department has divided its operational areas into the four locality planning areas used by Tayside Health Board. These four areas are managed by service managers who are responsible for all community care services except for those for people with learning disabilities. These are managed on an authority-wide basis.

2 Perth & Kinross Council make available a range of residential and, where appropriate, nursing home care, in addition to domiciliary, day and respite care services. Some of these services are provided directly by the council itself, others are purchased from the private or voluntary sectors.

3 Perth & Kinross has no local authority provision of day care for people with physical disabilities, and it is anticipated that a small number of Perth & Kinross residents will continue to use the specialist facility provided in Dundee. The council provides three Adult Resource Centres, which offer day care services to people with learning disabilities. The voluntary sector provides one day centre for people with mental health problems whilst the local authority provides an average of 50 day care places for this group in rural parts of its area. Specialist provision for people with substance misuse problems is mainly provided by the voluntary sector.

4 The Community Care Plan for Perth & Kinross estimates that within the area there are:

3,100 adults (age 16-64) with a severe or very severe physical disability;

400 adults with learning disabilities, of whom 100 have multiple disabilities;

3,100 adults with a severe mental illness;

2,040 adults at high risk of alcohol dependency;

500 adults who are injecting drugs.

NEEDS AND PROVISION FOR OLDER PEOPLE

5 The Perth & Kinross Community Care Action Plan also estimates that in 1994 there were some 10,200 people over the age of 75 within the area. This figure was based on data provided by the General Register Office (Scotland). Estimates from the same source indicate that the number of older people over 85 has increased to over 2,500 persons, compared to 2,200 in 1990.

6 Using these data, and employing the Intervals of Need model developed by Isaacs[22], we estimated that of all older people, aged 75 and above in Perth & Kinross:

between 2,200 and 3,600 require intensive levels of support, throughout the day and night;

between 300 and 1,100 require regular support several times a day;

between 1,400 and 2,800 require help solely with domestic tasks once a day or less.

7 The difference between the smaller and larger numbers depends on the amount of support older people obtain from their family, or other carers. If no families in Perth & Kinross were prepared or able to support those older people who require intensive levels of support, 3600 older people would have to obtain their support from public agencies.

EXISTING PROVISION OF COMMUNITY CARE SERVICES FOR OLDER PEOPLE

8 Older people requiring intensive support may obtain it in either residential or community settings. Using the above figures based on Isaacs' model, and statistical information routinely provided to, or available to The Scottish Office, we estimated that for older people requiring intensive levels of support in Perth & Kinross, in 1995/96:

a total of 287 "units of support"[23] were available, per 1000 people aged over 75 years;

less than half the available provision was within hospital (113 beds per 1000 people aged 75+);

residential and nursing homes provided over half the available places (150 beds per 1000 people aged 75+);

relatively few people received intensive support at home (24 people per 1000 people aged 75+ received a home help service 7 days per week).

9 These figures suggest that Perth & Kinross community care for older people who need intensive support, is provided by a mix of community-based and hospital services. There are few social care officers, or home help staff providing the intensive support older people and their families may require.

10 The same data suggest that older people with a need for regular support during the day may also experience difficulty in obtaining that support. Day care provision is less than the national average, and only a third of service users receive a home help service more than two days a week. In contrast the level of provision of meals, community alarms and aids to daily living are nearer to the national average.

11 On the basis of this data, it seems that the people who are best served by existing community care services are those older people who require assistance solely with domestic tasks. The home help service has been able to provide relatively short periods of support for those who need assistance with household tasks, shopping and the collection of pensions.

Residential and nursing home care

12 Table 11 below shows the places in residential and nursing homes when Perth & Kinross Council took over responsibility on 1st April 1996.

	No of Beds	Percent of Total	Occupancy (%)	Scotland (%)
Residential Homes				
Local Authority	226	15%	98	91
Private	312	20%	89	88
Voluntary	199	13%	80	92
Nursing Homes	794	52%	82	85
Total	1531	100%		

Table 11[24]: Residential and Nursing Home Beds in Perth & Kinross on 1st April 1996.

13 Local Authority residential home beds comprised 15% of the available bed spaces within the Perth & Kinross area as at 31 March 1996. This percentage declined to 11% when, in July this year, two local authority homes, with a total of 66 beds, were sold to a private sector home owner. There has been a decline in local authority beds for older people across Scotland during the last 10 years. Across all providers (local authority, private and voluntary sectors) the number of residential beds has recently shown a decrease, due in large part to conversion to single rooms in existing homes.

14 In contrast to residential homes, bed spaces in Scottish nursing homes have almost quadrupled in the last decade. Perth & Kinross, like Angus and Dundee, has reflected this trend. Occupancy rates, that is the number of residents compared with the number of beds, are continuing to fall in nursing homes, since although admission rates have increased slightly, the number of beds has increased at a faster rate.

15 Since 1 April, 1996 Perth & Kinross Council has been purchasing residential care in private and voluntary sector homes. Table 12 below shows the most recent pattern of admission to residential and nursing home care.

	No of Admissions	Percent of Total
Residential Homes		
Local Authority	0	0%
Private	11	23%
Voluntary	8	17%
Nursing Homes	29	60%
Total	48	100%

Table 12: Admissions to Residential and Nursing Home Care in Perth & Kinross 1.4.96 to 18.7.96.

16 The use made of private residential and nursing homes by Perth & Kinross Council has been the subject of complaint by private sector providers, who claim the local authority places people in local authority homes more readily. The above Table shows that out of a total of 48 placements since 1 April 1996, 60% were made to nursing homes (28 to private nursing homes and 1 to a voluntary nursing home) and 23% to private residential homes. No older people were admitted to the authority's own homes between 1 April 1996 and 18 July 1996 because of the plans to close two homes and the need to move residents from these homes to other homes of their own choice. There is clearly no bias against private or voluntary sector provision in placement patterns in Perth & Kinross.

Belmont Castle

17 Perth & Kinross Council purchase 8 registered residential care beds for people with dementia, and care support for 20 tenants in very sheltered housing in Belmont Castle. The arrangements between the Council and the lessees of the castle, The Church of Scotland, have been the subject of controversy prior to and during this inspection.

18 The Castle, which is owned by Dundee City Council, had operated as a residential care facility for older people for some 60 years. It is situated one mile from the village of Meigle, and some 15 miles from Dundee. The Castle has been refurbished to a high standard, at the expense of the Church of Scotland's Board of Social Responsibility. The accommodation now comprises a self contained dementia unit on the upper floor, 20 flatlets and a range of communal and office accommodation.

Dementia Unit

19 The development of the registered unit emerged from a specific approach taken towards the care of people with dementia by Tayside Regional Council and adopted by Perth & Kinross. This approach is based on the requirement for differing standards of support depending on the severity of the dementia. The policy of Perth & Kinross is that older people with moderate or severe dementia are not expected to be admitted to mainstream residential homes, unless there is a separate facility and an appropriate staffing ratio. Their policy is that older people with dementia and with behavioural problems, require continuing nursing care and should be admitted to "establishments which are registered with the Health Authority, either in part or in whole". Registered dementia units can attract payments by the Council of £322 per week. Nursing homes can attract payments of £295 per week. In addition, there are supplements of £10 for en suite facilities and £20 for small group living arrangements. Belmont Castle is the only registered dementia unit in Perth & Kinross.

20 We visited the unit and noted that it is located on the upper floor of the building. Residents access to other parts of the building and to the garden is by lift, with staff assistance. The unit is secured on the inside by an electronic keying system which is operated by staff. Residents are assisted in finding their way about the unit by signs on the toilets and the communal lounge/dining room. Nevertheless, some residents had difficulty in finding their way from their bedroom to the lounge. These drawbacks may inhibit the extent to which the unit can meet its full potential to provide a high quality of life to its residents.

Very Sheltered Housing Facility

21 The development of the very sheltered housing facilities within Belmont Castle has its origins in thinking within Tayside Regional Council. Intent on maintaining high levels of care and support for the older residents of the then registered home, but seeking to enhance the capacity of residents for maximum independent living, Tayside Regional Council agreed to fund that care when the residents changed their status to that of tenants. All new entrants to the flatlets will be provided with a tenancy agreement. New tenants will be accepted as an alternative to their entering a mainstream residential home for older people. Perth & Kinross Council have agreed to pay for a fixed number of hours for care staff. The cost is equivalent to £180 per tenant per week, but this sum does not take into account monies paid to tenants as Housing Benefit. This compares with a minimum of £203 payable for a residential bed in the independent sector.

22 In visiting the flatlets we noted that, while space and refurbishment standards were high, the sleeping areas were separated from living areas only by a partition (albeit attractive), due to building restrictions in force because Belmont Castle is a Listed Building. We noted that some tenants and some staff, unsurprisingly, continued to behave as if they were in a residential home. We noted that it was difficult for tenants to establish links with local shops and the post office because of the Castle's distance from local amenities. However, Belmont Castle does provide most attractive surroundings and in that respect is a joy for family and friends to visit.

23 We consider that Belmont Castle provides a good level of care to both tenants and residents. It is a resource which is consistent with the Council's wish to develop a wide range of different types of care provision, and we consider it provides value for money to the local authority when compared with the costs of its own residential care provision.

Day care

24 Perth & Kinross Council has one local authority day centre for older people. At 1st April 1996 the authority also provided day care within four residential units, one of which has since been sold. It also funds two voluntary sector centres, in Kinross and Blairgowrie.

25 The number of users of the local authority's day care services varies between 145 and 25 each week. During one week in our sample one residential home in a rural area provided day care support to just one person. The provision of meals, personal care and leisure activities are the principal services provided to users. The day centre is open 7 days a week, as is the day care service at one of the residential units. The day care service in other residential units is only available on weekdays.

26 The voluntary centres open 4 or 5 days a week. In Kinross the day centre provides support to 75 older people each week, including 5 people with dementia. The cost of the service to the local authority is said to be £4.07 per place per day. In Blairgowrie there are 62 users, at a cost to the Council of £2.50 per each user visit.

Home care

27 In May 1996 the home help service in Perth & Kinross remained a service provided to many older people, but for few hours. Over 75% of older people received the service for three hours or less each week. The service was geared mainly towards providing domestic support, rather than personal care. Less than 13% of people received personal care.

28 Perth & Kinross Council does not purchase home care from the private sector. It does contract with Crossroads to carry out a range of domestic/household and personal care tasks, mainly at evenings and weekends. The cost to the Council of this is said to be £8.79 per hour. In addition the Council's contract with the Church of Scotland, for Belmont Castle, specifies a mixture of domestic, household and personal tasks for the 20 tenants. This is costed at £6.25 per hour.

29 From information available to us, the provision of meals, both mobile and at lunch clubs appears to be above the Scottish average, as do the number of community alarms. Occupational therapy support – through the provision of aids to daily living, and advice on adaptations – is of average provision. The introduction of social care officers is an important contribution to providing intensive care at home. Sheltered housing, together with medium dependency housing is available to 10% of the population over 75.

THE QUALITY OF CARE IN RESIDENTIAL AND NURSING HOMES IN PERTH & KINROSS

Residential Homes

30 The quality of care in residential homes in the Perth & Kinross area was judged on the basis of the most recent annual inspection reports available at the time of the Inspection. We examined reports on 9 private, 6 voluntary and 2 local authority homes which had been submitted by Perth & Kinross. The inspection reports on the two local authority homes, like all but three of the other sector home inspections, were carried out by the former Tayside Region inspection unit. (See Appendix 4, for details of the legislative context and standard setting)

31 We also looked at reports provided by Tayside Health Board in relation to five nursing homes in Perth & Kinross.

32 Our analysis of reports provided by Perth & Kinross showed that the local authority homes had previously met the lowest average percentage of staffing standards. However, since 1 April 1996, the new authority has taken steps to ensure that their homes have the necessary budgets to meet all the staffing standards. The two inspection reports on local authority homes we examined had both been undertaken before 1 April 1996, and so do not reflect the current staffing position. Our analysis also shows that the independent sector homes in Perth & Kinross meet, overall, a higher percentage of standards.

33 Figure 7 below shows the average percentage of standards met by homes across the sectors. These percentages were calculated by taking the number of standards met as a proportion of the total number applied in each section of every inspection report and dividing the total by the number of homes in each sector. The total average was calculated

by adding the number of standards met by the homes in each sector and expressing this as a percentage of the total number of standards.

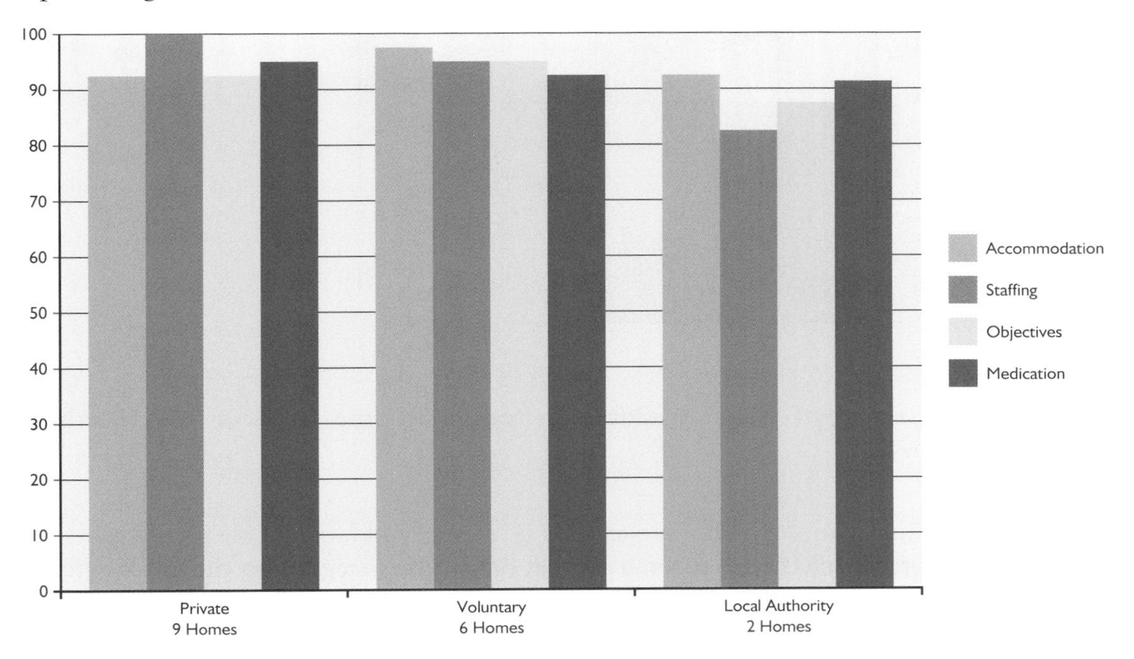

Figure 7: Average Percentage of Standards Met in Residential Homes by Sector in Perth & Kinross.

34 There was widespread evidence from local inspection unit interviews with a sample of residents that they were generally unaware of their rights, whether this concerned the written contract with the home, access to their care plan and their right to participate in its construction or the right to a choice at mealtimes and to be consulted about menu planning generally. Individual homes had not always carried out structural work called for in previous inspections, such as installation of a lift or providing additional sitting rooms or bathrooms, all of which have capital as well as revenue cost implications. The standards place great emphasis on written policies and adherence to procedures and the process of care.

35 Being able to make choices is as important to older people in homes as it is to everyone else. One very important choice is that of being able to choose not to share a bedroom with someone else. Figure 8 below shows that the Council homes offer significantly more choice in this regard. For all sectors the proportion of beds available as single rooms is high and reflects increasingly higher overall standards of provision in residential care.

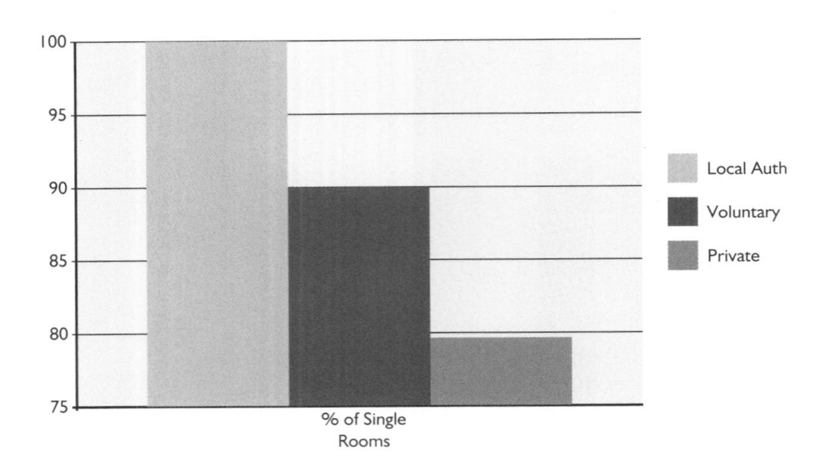

Figure 8: Percentage of Beds Available in Single Rooms By Sector in Perth & Kinross.

36 Choices about planning your care and about menus and food are also important. We undertook a more detailed analysis on a sub-set of standards regarding the availability of these choices. We also analysed the reports to compare the standards regarding older people's involvement in the construction of their care plans, whether their individual likes and dislikes about food were taken into account by homes and whether they were involved in or consulted about menu planning.

37 Table 13 below shows the number of homes which met the standards across the sectors.

Standard	Local Authority	Private	Voluntary
Care Plan involvement 2.28,2.31,2.32,2.35 or 2.36	Met in 1 out of 2 homes.	Met in all 9 homes.	Met in all 6 homes.
Menu Planning Involvement 2.60, 2.63,2.66,2.67,2.70, 2.71or 2.72.	Met in 1 out of 2 homes.	Met in 7 out of 9 homes.	Met in all 6 homes.
Individual food preferences met 2.61,2.64,2.67,2.68, 2.71 2.72 or 2.73	Met in 1 out of 2 homes.	Met in all 9 homes.	Met in all 6 homes.

Note: The numbering given to the same standards varied between individual inspection reports, both within and across authorities. This is indicated at Column 1 of the Table.

Table 13: Proportion of Homes in Each Sector Meeting Selected Standards on Choices in Perth & Kinross.

38 The small size of the local authority sample makes comparisons between sectors difficult, particularly since Perth & Kinross Council has acted swiftly to remedy the problem with staffing levels in local authority homes identified above. Had it been possible to include all the local authority and registered homes in the analysis, the performance levels may have been different. The analysis suggests that, in this sample, independent sector homes met most of the standards we associated with quality of life. However, in respect of one of the most important standards, to do with privacy, the local authority did best, having only single rooms in its homes. The proportion of single rooms was lowest in the private sector.

39 Local inspection unit reports highlighted both minor and major shortfalls in homes. These ranged from minor shortfalls in standards such as resident signatures on care plans, the updating of brochures and the revision of admission procedures, to major issues such as substantial upgrading of the building. Where such upgrading or alteration of the building was required, a three year period was allowed for the standard to be met. In many cases, this is not until 1998.

Nursing Homes

40 Our conclusions about quality in nursing homes were based on reports of recently conducted inspections carried out by Health Board staff in a sample of five nursing homes in Perth & Kinross.

41 Comments by Tayside Health Board inspectors regarding the quality of care in these nursing homes ranged from 'favourable' to 'generally favourable', except for one home where the standard was particularly low and many issues required immediate action. These issues included a large number of complaints from both staff and residents regarding the quality of the food, particularly at the evening meal. Again, some aspects of the medication procedures and practices required attention in all five homes and two of them required a significant number of repairs and refurbishment, such as attention to damaged paintwork and broken sash cords on windows. Inspectors recommended that the owners of one home should invest in some pressure-relieving aids. Two of the five homes were inadequately staffed and a further two homes recorded as many as 111 and 112 minor accidents in the preceding 12 months.

42 There are a number of quality issues highlighted in the inspection reports on this sample of nursing homes in Perth & Kinross, relating to aspects of the buildings themselves and extending to important elements of daily life for residents, as well as staff, such as meals. The lower than registration standard staffing levels in two homes and the high number of recorded minor accidents in them suggest that these unmet standards are having a measurable, negative effect on the quality of life of residents. Such factors serve to highlight the importance of adequately staffed homes and the vulnerability of older people living in them if staffing levels are not maintained.

43 At present Tayside Health Board does not make Nursing Home inspection reports available to the local authority.

THE FRAILTY OF OLDER PEOPLE LIVING IN RESIDENTIAL AND NURSING HOMES IN PERTH & KINROSS.

44 We compared frailty levels in two distinct kinds of provision, residential homes and nursing homes, as well as between sectors. We used information about frailty in residential homes which is routinely submitted to The Scottish Office on an annual basis. We examined these data in relation to all the local authority homes, and a random, but broadly representative sample of homes run by the private and voluntary sectors. Finally we examined nursing home inspection reports provided to us by Tayside Health Board.

45 Our sample in Perth & Kinross comprised 4 local authority residential homes, 8 private residential homes, 2 voluntary residential homes and 5 nursing homes.

46 We looked at 3 types of frailty: incontinence; people who are bed or chair-bound; people who are "confused". The definition of "confusion" adopted by SWSG when requesting statistical returns from local authorities refers to people "whose mental confusion arises from brain pathology and is of permanent and irreversible nature, and who require regular supervision or help to perform tasks of daily living, or constant care because of aimless wandering etc." The definition of confusion used by medical staff when someone is admitted to a nursing home, or by a visiting member of an inspection team may be different.

47 All nursing homes in the sample had between a third (38%) and over a half (58%) of residents with incontinence. Two homes showed markedly higher levels of "confusion" and of chair or bedbound residents, and the 3 homes which showed high levels of "confusion" each had more than half their residents with this degree of frailty, rising to almost three-quarters (74%) in one home.

48 Residents of local authority homes do not have high levels of frailty measured by any of our 3 criteria. Levels of confusion are less than 50% in all homes, and the rate of incontinence ranges from 11 – 26%, well below the lowest rate (38%) in the nursing home sample.

49 The sample of randomly selected private residential homes in Perth & Kinross shows a very mixed picture of frailty. Half the homes have 50% or more of their residents who are "confused", whilst 2 homes do not have any residents so described. The incidence of incontinence is also varied, with half the homes having no residents described as incontinent. Those homes which do have residents with incontinence problems have them in similar proportions to the local authority homes.

50 The voluntary homes in Perth & Kinross are similar in their levels of people with incontinence. The levels of "confusion", which range from 11 – 25%, are lower than those private homes which have numbers of confused residents, and slightly lower than the range in local authority homes. Levels of incontinence are similar to those in residential homes in the other sectors.

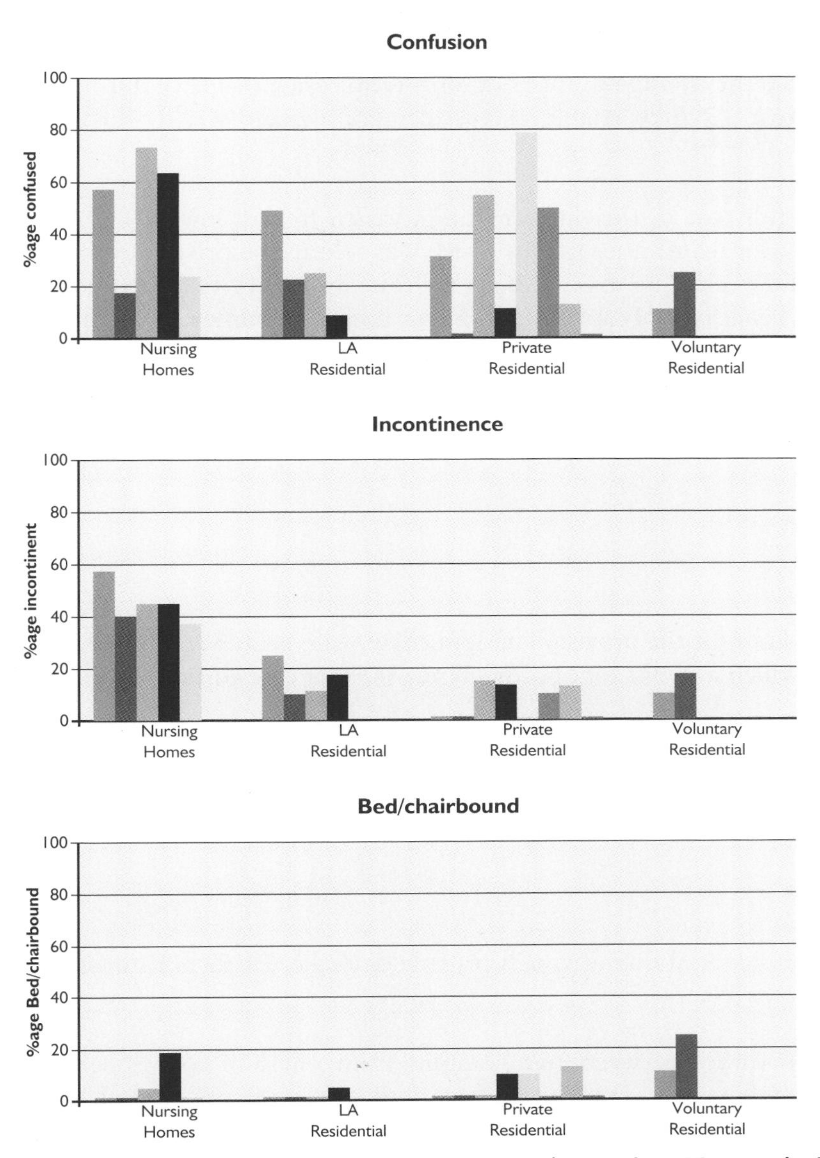

Figure 9: Frailty levels in Residential and Nursing Homes in Perth & Kinross

COSTS OF COMMUNITY CARE SERVICES

Local Authority Residential Care

51 Currently, within Perth & Kinross Council, there are 4 local authority residential homes: Parkdale, Dalweem and North Inch Homes which provide both residential and day care, and Beechgrove Home which provides residential care only. In addition, Belmont Castle, run by the Church of Scotland, provides residential dementia care and very sheltered housing.

52 As with the other unitary authorities, we calculated the actual costs of each of these units, using figures supplied by the Councils themselves, and applying the current costing formula and guidance issued by COSLA and CIPFA, where appropriate. (See Appendix 2,

Notes to Costs Analysis and Appendix 3 for a full list of costs). We agreed with the local authority that we would use the average number of long-term residents (160) during the period 1 April – 31 August 1996 to enable us to calculate average weekly costs per resident.

53 The average weekly full cost in the different units varied from a low of £302 per resident week (in one of the local authority homes which was sold to the private sector), to a high of £403 per resident week. The main reasons for this divergence related to varied levels of capital value (and hence cost of capital) in different homes and differing occupancy rates. The cost of the most expensive home can be attributed to the low occupancy level within this home; we have been informed by Council management that in the first few months of 1996 the occupancy within this home was deliberately kept low so that residents from Catmoor and Strathtay Homes, which both closed on 4 July 1996, could be transferred if they so chose.

Domiciliary Care

54 The average cost per hour for the provision of domiciliary care is £6.32. Most of these costs relate to staff costs, which account for approximately 90% of care costs.

55 In its Community Care Action Plan, the local authority states that the full cost of its home care service, based on the provision of the former Tayside Regional Council in 1995/96, is £6.50 per day.

Day Care

56 In addition to the 3 residential homes which provide day care, Perth & Kinross also has one day care centre, Lewis Place.

57 Day care costs also fluctuated between units, ranging from a high of £60.33 per user per day, to a low of £8.55 per user per day. This wide variation has been largely caused by the staff to older person ratio and opening times. One home, for example, provides day care seven days per week with low utilisation levels at the weekend and therefore its staff costs per older person are much higher than a unit which is only opening five days per week. In addition, costs of capital have not been included in the calculation for homes where residential care is also given, as we were informed that the premises/capital costs of providing this additional care are minimal. The weighted average cost of local authority day care per user per day is £35.08.

58 The Perth & Kinross Community Care Action Plan gives the cost of day care as £22 per day, based on the provision of the former Tayside Regional Council in 1995/96.

Performance against Standard Rate

59 Section 22 of the National Assistance Act 1948 requires local authorities to set a standard rate for local authority residential care within their area; this amount should equate to the actual costs to the local authority of providing the care. Perth & Kinross have performed against their published standard rate as follows :

	Standard Rate	Average Cost Calculated
Residential Care	£362/week	£375.18/week

60 The Council's published standard rate is below the average full cost.

Comparative Costs and Potential Savings

61 Currently, within Perth & Kinross, independent sector providers are paid at a rate of £203 per week for residential care, although various premiums are added for different care packages. The figure of £223.62, used in the Table below, is the average cost paid to the independent sector by the local authority, taking account of these premiums. The original figures were supplied by the Council.

62 Eligible residents placed in the independent sector receive from the Department of Social Security a Residential Allowance of £54.00 per week; this £54.00 is remitted to the local authority. No similar allowance is received by individuals placed in a local authority home. In addition, dependent on which sector the resident is in, a different level of income support is available. We have not included Attendance Allowances payable in the first four weeks, due to their marginal impact on costing.

63 Table 14 below shows the costs to Perth & Kinross Council of placing a resident in an independent sector home compared with the average costs of maintaining places in their own homes.

	Local Authority £	Independent £
Gross average cost per resident to local authority/price paid per resident by local authority	375.18	223.62
Less : Income received by local authority		
Residential Allowance	–	(54.00)
Income Support Premiums (Note 1[25])	–	(23.23)
Income Support (Note 2[26])	(48.00)	(34.15)
Net cost to local authority	**327.18**	**112.24**

Table 14: Comparative Costs to Perth & Kinross Council of Local Authority Provision and Purchase from Independent Sector of Residential Care.

64 Table 14 shows that Perth & Kinross Council could make savings by placing more residents in the independent sector. To identify the scale of the potential gross savings available to the local authority it is first necessary to consider costs that would not be saved. These fall into three areas.

65 First, some overhead costs and a proportion of the cost of capital would not be saved.

66 Secondly, the costs of effecting the closure of homes need to be taken into account. Closure of further local authority homes would either require redeployment of staff within the authority, or redundancies, or transfer to new providers. Each of these options would to some extent limit the savings which could be made. If further homes were sold to private or voluntary sector providers the new owners might take on existing staff from the homes. These staff would, of course, be covered by the application of the Transfer of Undertakings (Protection of Employment) Regulations 1981, and it is possible, indeed likely, that new owners would be reluctant to accept such transfers. The new owners of the homes which Perth & Kinross closed earlier this year did not accept any staff on transfer.

67 The cost in the early years of closing or transfering homes to the independent sector might very substantially reduce the savings realised, particularly if redundancy costs all fell in the first year. In addition, and depending on the arrangements made, local authorities might not benefit from the £54 DSS income until the new provision had been established for some years.

68 Thirdly, a number of factors might contribute to rises in the price of places in the independent sector and thus further reduce the potential savings. To bring all the independent sector provision up to the standard of the Council's own provision in respect of single room accommodation would be likely to lead to price increases. Moreover it is arguable that the price charged to the Council by private and voluntary homes is artificially low and can only be sustained by higher charges made for privately financed placements and by some 'hidden costs' of services charged for particular services provided to individual residents. If the proportion of privately and publicly financed placements changed then arguably the charge to the Council could rise. Independent sector bodies have argued strongly that the prices paid by the Council are not sufficient.

69 It is not possible to quantify the effects of these diverse elements and a reasonable judgement must be made. It would be unrealistic for the Council to envisage that it could make savings proportionate to the variation in weekly cost given in Table 14. Nevertheless, we consider that the Council could make more effective use of its resources by making greater use of independent sector provision and that realistically the potential savings could be between £780,000 and £1.5 million which could be otherwise applied to enhance community care services[27].

70 We were advised by Perth & Kinross that the local authority saved £370,000 as a result of the closure of two of its homes in July 1996. The Council avoided the cost problems associated with redeployment or redundancy, which are outlined above, by either freezing residential vacancies elsewhere or by recruiting temporary staff during the "shadow year" of the authority, and leading up to the sale of the two homes. In examining the scope for further savings, Perth & Kinross will need to consider whether and how this can be achieved again. Perth & Kinross Council argues that the local authority must maintain some public sector provision to enable it to act as the "provider of last resort". This is a reasonable view, although it is possible that "last resort" provision could be negotiated with independent sector providers. The Council also argues that it must maintain some direct provision in order to meet statutory responsibilities under section 59 of the Social Work (Scotland) Act 1968. We do not accept this view. Section 59 places a duty on the local authority to "provide and maintain such residential and other establishments as may be required.......or to arrange for the provision of such establishments". This clearly allows for indirect provision of services from other providers.

71 These considerations point to ensuring that a realistic view is taken of potential savings and careful management of any changes. Managing any substantial change in services for vulnerable people requires great care on the part of the local authority and may only be achieved successfully over a period of time. The authority must plan its change strategy well, must allow sufficient time for implementation, and must communicate its intentions to service users and carers, to their own staff and to the wider public, in a way which is both informative and reassuring about the continuing care which will be available. This requires local authorities to make a realistic appraisal of the most cost-efficient mixed economy for their area, and to plan a strategy to achieve this within a realistic timescale.

Budget Setting and Control

72 Our review of Perth & Kinross Council's budgetary control mechanisms for 1996/97 identified that budgets had been incrementally set using as the base year a disaggregated Tayside Regional Council budget. There had been a need to set a budget quickly for the new Unitary Council, which was why the Council had developed an incrementally based budget for 1996/97. We noted that the use of incremental budget setting was again to be deployed for the 1997/98 budget.

73 At present, within Perth & Kinross Council, the current level of delegation is to service managers on the purchasing side with individual unit managers on the provider side having their own allocated budgets. The purchase of residential and nursing home care is not delegated, but held centrally; this level of central control is thought necessary by management at a time when spending is to be reduced.

74 We were informed that the continued development of the K2 computerised client database system will eventually lead to the alignment of current financial and management information systems. However, this is unlikely to occur within the next four to five years.

Planning and purchasing

75 The revised Community Care Action Plan (1996/97) for Perth & Kinross is an update of the Community Care Plan originally prepared by the former Tayside Regional Council in conjunction with Tayside Health Board. Information contained in that earlier document was disaggregated at the level of each the new authorities. The plan has been modified by Perth & Kinross Council in a number of ways. For example it contains strategic objectives concerning assessment and care management and carers.

76 The Plan provides a set of broad brush statements about planned actions in relation to identified objectives, indicates which agencies are responsible for taking these forward, the funding source (where applicable) and the target date by which the action is to be achieved. It also provides a considerable amount of quite detailed statistical information about needs indicators for the range of community care groups, population sizes and other relevant data.

77 The Plan does not, however, contain a clear statement about the Council's purchasing intention, although information is provided about the pattern of purchasing of residential and nursing home care in that area during the previous year. Senior officers of Perth & Kinross Social Work Department informed us that this would be remedied in the new

Plan, to be published in April 1997. The minute of a departmental meeting, supplied to us by the authority, confirmed that the authority's commitment to meet all the requirements of the Direction on Purchasing. A draft of the 1997-2000 Community Care Plan, which is currently out for consultation has made very good progress towards meeting this requirement.

78 Despite providing an impressive amount of statistical data in relation to current services and estimated prevalence rates, the plan makes little attempt to relate this information with a view to the identification of service shortfalls. It does not contain specific information about expected levels and volumes of service to be provided or purchased over the planning period, nor does it set out clear outputs and outcomes associated with the planned actions. Finally, the Plan lacks any information about the financial resources and assumption underpinning the planned actions.

79 The Community Care Plan is not the only expression of joint planning activity. Tayside Health Board has been active with Perth & Kinross Council (together with Angus and Dundee) in establishing the framework within which resources transferred from the Health Board would be made available to the Council. The framework includes draft agreements on definitions of continuing health care, hospital discharge arrangements and the disaggregation of Resource Transfer.

80 There has, hitherto, been no resource transfer to Perth & Kinross Council. The Scottish Health Advisory Service (SHAS) in a report in February 1996 noted that, at that time, "no transfer of resources [had taken place] despite the balance of care having shifted from hospital care." The SHAS report reiterated concerns about the geriatric service in Perth indicating that Hillside Hospital was "no longer a suitable place for continuing care for older people."

81 During our discussions with Mr Young, Director of Commissioning and Strategic Management for Tayside Health Board, we were told that Tayside Health Board anticipates that £19m. will be transferred to the three authorities during the current 4-year programme. This will allow for 550 bed closures across the Board's area. £468,000 had been set aside for resource transfer in 1996/97 to Perth & Kinross. Agreement has also been reached in principle for the transfer of up to 20 places from Hillside, based on agreed joint assessment work, which will transfer between £400,000 – £500,000 to the local authority.

82 The Health Board took a decision to phase their work on resource transfer, starting in Angus , then Dundee and finally in Perth & Kinross. This decision was based on their assessment of the preparedness of local NHS teams to take part in the multi-agency planning required to achieve the transfers.

83 Perth & Kinross has agreed a set of joint planning structures with its planning partners, which reflects the detailed guidance issued by SWSG. The process is based on a main 3-tier structure, the work of which is further informed by a number of associated service-based groups, an existing locality planning group (based in the North West Perthshire) and the Housing Forum. Users and carers, and independent sector providers will be represented on both the Joint Planning and Policy Development Group – which is charged with formulating the Community Care Plan, and on the Joint Member Group which is responsible for agreeing the structure and content of the Plan. The staff and officers attending the groups will all be at a sufficiently high level within their organisations to be able to commit resources on behalf of those agencies.

Purchasing

84 A senior officer and the Director of Social Work, Mrs Bridgeford, both stated that the Council did not have any specific policy in relation to the purchase of services from the private sector, although there was said to be substantial voluntary sector activity within the area.

85 Although the current Community Care Action Plan does not contain a clear statement of the council's purchasing intentions, the senior officer with responsibility for planning indicated in interview that the new Plan would contain a clear statement of the Council's purchasing intentions. We were told that the Social Work Department is at present developing a philosophy and a set of principles to underpin a purchasing strategy to be linked to care specifications for each area of service.

86 We have been made aware recently that Perth & Kinross are circulating a draft of their 1997-2000 Community Care Plan. We have not examined this document in detail but we have received comments from the private sector in Perth & Kinross that there are new policy initiatives in the draft which they welcome.

87 The local authority has historically been the primary provider of both day and domiciliary care, although some domiciliary care is currently purchased from the voluntary sector. We were advised that this position was likely to change over the next few years. The senior officer indicated his expectation that in the future Perth & Kinross would go out to tender for the care elements of all new services, a view which appeared to represent a logical extension of the current position as reflected in the minute of the first meeting of the Commissioning and Implementation Group, one of the new planning groups.

IMPACT OF REGULATION AND CHARGING

Inspection and registration

88 On reorganisation, Perth & Kinross Council established its own inspection and registration unit. It is responsible for registering residential and day care establishments for children and adults in the independent sector and for inspecting all establishments, including those of Perth & Kinross Council. The Council has adopted the standards developed by Tayside Regional Council, but the Director of Social Work has indicated that she wishes to review those standards by February 1997.

89 In their submission to us, Perth & Kinross state that the inherited standards are prescriptive. It is intended that a new set of standards will be formulated. The standards will be "concise, realistic....and reflecting users' needs." The submission acknowledges there had been a "history of some considerable hostility between providers of all sectors and the Quality Assurance Unit." The submission then details a number of ways in which anticipated changes should resolve this hostility.

90 Mrs Bridgeford spoke of recent initiatives to improve consultation with providers. These have been welcomed by providers with whom we spoke. In particular, providers have welcomed the sharing of information relevant to their interests.

Charging for non-residential services

91 In common with the other two successor authorities to the former Tayside Region, Perth & Kinross had been forced to introduce charges for non-residential care services in an attempt to reduce a financial shortfall. Without the introduction of charges, the Social Work Department would have been required to cut services by a further £0.5m. Domiciliary charges are based on a calculation of the actual hourly cost of these services and on an assessment of the users' income. Services are provided free to individuals with an assessable income of less than £90 per week, and to couples with an assessable income of less than £125 per week.

92 Existing service users were advised of the intention to introduce charges by letter, and were offered a welfare benefits check to ensure that they were in receipt of their full benefits entitlement. The information also informed users of the Director of Social Work's power to reduce or waive charges in certain circumstances. We were advised that this power had been exercised in a number of cases. Subsequently all service users were sent letters containing details of their financial assessment, the charge applied and the level of service to be delivered.

93 We were told that as a result of the benefits checks introduced in tandem with the charging policy, over £1,000,000 additional benefits have been claimed by the people of Perth & Kinross.

94 It was acknowledged that the introduction of charges had caused a number of problems, with anticipated difficulties being exacerbated by delays in issuing bills. The first bills were issued in June, although it is intended that they should be issued monthly in arrears, and were found to be uninformative and confusing.

95 The authority has since taken a number of steps to improve the situation. An improved billing system, with more information, is now in place. A policy decision has also been taken by the department that where an individual's assessment has not been completed timeously by the local authority, bills in respect of that user's services will not be backdated further than two charging periods (i.e. a maximum of eight weeks). Finally, the local authority has set up a telephone helpline, for four months, to provide advice and information to service users about the charging policy.

96 The department intends to monitor the impact of charges through an examination of take-up and drop-out rates, but will also follow up some of those former users who have refused services since the introduction of charges, because of concerns about the level of risk such people might be exposed to.

The views of service users in Perth & Kinross

97 We asked a sample of residential and nursing home residents, and users of domiciliary care services in their own homes and in very sheltered housing about the amount of information and choice they were given when deciding on these forms of care. We spoke to 16 people in residential care, 6 people in nursing homes, 12 very sheltered housing tenants and 10 people who were users of domiciliary services in their own homes. We also received questionnaires from 5 carers. None of the people we spoke to in residential care was in a local authority home. The local authority had made no placements into its own homes since 1 April 1996 because two homes were to be closed.

Residential Care

98 The most common reason for a move to residential care amongst this sample of older people was health needs, which were mentioned by 13 of the 16 people interviewed. Four residents had considered other ways of meeting his or her needs, mostly through domiciliary care services (3 people) or, in one case, through an application for sheltered housing, which was still being considered.

99 Amongst this sample, most residents had heard of the home through a professional: 3 had been told about it by a social worker and 7 by health professionals (either their G.P, in 4 cases, or hospital staff, in 3 cases).

100 Few of the residents recalled being given information to help them choose a home. Only 2 remembered being given either written or verbal information, whilst 6 said they were given no information and a further 6 were unsure. No response was recorded from two other residents. Less than half the sample (7) of people interviewed in private or voluntary sector care homes had been offered a choice of homes, whilst 4 others said that they had not. Three people were not sure about this point.

101 Just over half (9) of the 16 people in private or voluntary homes had received either written or verbal information about the charges for residential care, as had the carers of three other people. Five residents had been told about the possibility of "topping up" fees, if the home they wanted charged more than the local authority would pay, and 2 had not been advised of this. Four residents were partly self-financing. Only one person, in private sector care, indicated that charges had been an important factor influencing their choice of home.

Nursing Homes

102 Six people were in the nursing home sample in Perth & Kinross, all in private nursing homes, including one that was jointly registered with social work as a residential home. They gave the same reason for their move as the people in residential homes. Unlike the former group, none had considered other means of meeting their needs. None of the people in this sample had heard of their home from a social worker, although 2 had been told about the homes by their G.P.

103 Little information was given to users and carers about the choice of homes available to them and about charges. Only one person recalled being given information to help make the choice of home. Three people had been offered a choice of homes in the private and voluntary sectors. One private sector resident and one carer of a person in a voluntary sector nursing home had been given verbal information about charges, whilst one resident had been given written information. Three residents had been told about the possibility of "topping up" fees. Half of the sample (3 people) were partly self-funding, and one person was totally self-financing, yet only one person had considered charges to be an important factor influencing choice of home.

Very Sheltered Housing

104 Twelve tenants of very sheltered housing were interviewed in Perth & Kinross. Eight resided in Belmont Castle, run by the Church of Scotland, and 4 at Quayside Court, run by Bield Housing Association. Health was mentioned as the main reason for moving into very sheltered housing by 5 people, whilst others mentioned not wanting to burden carers, their own homes no longer being suitable or not being able to cope at home anymore as the reason for their move. All 5 tenants who said health issues were the cause of their move lived in Belmont Castle, and had all been resident before it became very sheltered housing.

105 Half of the 8 Belmont Castle tenants had originally heard of the facility from hospital or community medical staff, one had heard about it from a social worker, and another from the minister at the local hospital. One of the tenants of Quayside Court had heard of it from a social worker, the others knew of it by reputation or from family members.

106 Only 2 tenants, one in Quayside Court and one in Belmont Castle, had considered residential or nursing home care, whilst 7 others said they had never considered these options.

107 All 4 tenants living at Quayside Court had been receiving services to help them at home before they moved into very sheltered housing: 3 people had had home helps (one also had the community nurse visiting) and one person received meals on wheels.

108 The tenants of both very sheltered housing schemes received considerable help with daily living from staff of the schemes, although the people in Belmont Castle generally needed help with more activities than those in Quayside Court. All the Belmont Castle tenants needed help with dressing and managing medication, compared with only half (2) of those interviewed in Quayside Court. In addition to help from very sheltered housing staff, all but one tenant, who was in Belmont Castle, were receiving at least one community service.

109 We asked tenants whether there had been any changes to the services they received since 1st April 1996. Two of the Belmont Castle tenants said that the building had been refurbished and that they now had tenancy agreements, whilst another stated that there had been no change. The remaining 5 tenants either did not know or their answer was not recorded. Of the 4 Quayside Court tenants, 3 stated that the only change was that charges had been introduced. Two of these people said that they had received no information about the charges, one had received written information and one had received verbal information from a social worker. None of the tenants in either establishment considered charges to be a significant factor in deciding what additional services they would use.

110 Two Belmont Castle tenants were clear that they had been offered a choice of services, 3 said that they had not, and 3 did not know. Three of the Quayside Court tenants said they had been offered a choice, whilst one had not.

Domiciliary Services

111 We interviewed 10 people in Perth & Kinross who were living in their own homes and receiving 10 or more hours of home help a week. Eight of these people lived alone but half of them had support from a family carer. Half of the people interviewed had found out about the community care services available to them from their GP or hospital staff. Two people had contacted the Social Work Department themselves and a relative had done so for a third.

112 Half the service users had been given a choice about the kinds of services they would use. Three people had not been given a choice and the others were unsure. Four people were sure that they had not been offered a choice of agency to provide a particular service; the others were uncertain. The domiciliary users were receiving between one and 7 different community care services. The median number of services being received by this group was five. Everybody had home help, the amount ranging between 6.5 and 14 hours a week, and all but one user was paying for this. Two people were also using private home help. Four people had meals on wheels between 2 and 5 times a week, one of whom also attended a lunch club twice a week. The community nursing service was visiting 6 people, the frequency of visits varying between twice weekly and bi-monthly. Four people had been provided with a community alarm. Two people went to day care once or twice a week for which they paid a minimum charge to cover meals.

113 Half of the interviewees remembered being given written information about the introduction of charges for community care services to people at home, and the same proportion thought the cost was 'important' or 'very important' in influencing their decisions about what services to accept.

114 The users were asked about the activities of daily living with which they needed assistance. Most people (7) interviewed needed help with the majority of activities. All 10 people needed help with at least 6 activities and one person required help with 12 activities. Despite the services being provided, 6 people still needed more help in some areas of their lives – more than one in most cases. Half of these people needed more help with gardening and half needed more help with personal care. Others needed a ramp installed and others a window cleaning service.

115 Despite significant levels of disability, only one person had tried residential or nursing home care as an alternative to remaining at home, on the advice of her GP but was unable to settle. Two people would be prepared to consider such a move "in the future" and one person's family had already suggested it to them.

Chapter 5

Conclusions and Recommendations

1 In this chapter our conclusions for each Council are grouped under common headings. Angus, Dundee City and Perth & Kinross Councils quite rightly take distinctively different approaches to how best to meet the needs of the people they serve. We have described their uniqueness in the preceding chapters and we have reached conclusions specific to each Council. We bring these together in this chapter because there are some common elements and we believe there are important findings for all social work authorities in these conclusions.

2 We have grouped our findings from this inspection under the following headings:

- Quality of Care and Standards;
- Value for Money;
- The Planning, Provision and Purchasing of Services;
- Information.

Quality of care and Standards

We concluded that residential homes in all sectors were generally providing a good quality of care and, for the most part, meeting the standards laid down by Angus, Dundee and Perth & Kinross. A minority of homes have staffing levels below the requirements of registration. We consider that the standards should be revised to provide an improved focus on the quality of care that residents receive and on the quality of their lives.

3 The purpose of standard-setting is twofold. Standards describe the nature and quality of care that service users can expect; and, they set benchmarks against which the performance of service providers is able to be judged. Standards are set by local authorities, for residential homes, and by Health Boards for nursing homes. Achieving a consensus over what constitutes 'high quality' in residential care is not an easy task.

4 The inspection standards developed by the former Tayside Regional Council and initially adopted by Angus, Dundee City and Perth & Kinross Councils are numerous, prescriptive, process-driven, and seek to avoid risk to residents and providers alike. Meeting some standards will not, of itself, deliver high quality care. In some cases, compliance with the letter rather than the spirit of the standard may actually be detrimental to resident autonomy.

5 The single-room standard is one among over 300 standards applied to residential homes in the 3 Councils' areas. The research literature[28] on users' views has identified that the vast majority of people in residential care wish to have their own bedroom, in order to

safeguard their privacy. Where couples want to share then they should be able to do so with access to a separate additional room as is provided in all the Council homes and most of the independent homes. For most people in both local authority and independent sector residential care in Angus, Dundee and Perth & Kinross this is now a reality and is to be applauded. We found many other standards to be helpful, reflecting what most older people consider important. However, there are others which are concerned with meeting procedures which may not be associated with judgements about the quality of care for residents. In some instances, meeting the standard may result in inflexibility and a limiting of residents' independence. Prescriptive standards can inhibit creative and flexible models of care. Standards should be used to demonstrate good quality care, not whether a procedure has been carried out.

6 Older people who are reluctant to enter residential care cite loss of independence as one of their main fears. Independence or autonomy implies an ability to make choices and to run risks. Standards for residential care should address risk constructively as a part of 'normal' living and seek to manage and minimise it rather than eliminate or avoid it. The majority of older people who move into residential homes are very competent, retaining their mental skills despite increasing frailty, and with a lifetime of decision-making to draw on when assessing potentially risky behaviour. High quality care should enable rather than inhibit their autonomy.

7 There are at present no nationally accepted standards for registration of residential homes. A recent report[29] has recommended that the Scottish Office establish a national consultative group with the primary task of devising and promoting nationally recommended guidelines and quality of care standards. The report states that the welfare of each resident is central to the registration scheme. We agree with this statement and commend it and the recommendations in the report.

Angus

8 Angus Council submitted its revised standards for adult residential care, with a statement of its philosophy of care. We welcome this initiative. The statement puts due emphasis on the importance of providing high quality accommodation and care to service users. The inspection checklist seeks to achieve such high quality by laying down the Council's criteria by which this may be achieved. However, the checklist puts great emphasis on the existence of and compliance with procedures. Many of the procedures are bureaucratic and related to statutory obligation or organisational liability, rather than having a proven relationship to high quality provision.

9 Local authority homes in Angus did not meet as many of the present inspection standards as homes provided by the independent sector, although they did have the highest percentage of single rooms. Angus Council acted swiftly to improve staffing levels in their own homes with effect from 1 April 1996, and we welcome this. Since some local authority homes have high proportions of mentally frail residents, any shortfall in staffing levels is likely to have implications for the quality of care staff are able to give.

10 Some nursing homes in Angus are also caring for high proportions of very frail people. The buildings and fabric of some homes are below registration standards and some have high incidences of accidents to residents. Whilst it is impossible to ensure that no residents

have accidents, where frail and vulnerable groups of older people are cared for, it is particularly important that required standards relating to staffing levels should be met. In our view, joint or collaborative work between the local authority and health board inspection units could assist in raising the standard of residential provision for older people overall. We were told by Angus Council that they are keen to develop joint working on inspection with Tayside Health Board.

Dundee

11 Using the standards and indicators developed by the former Tayside Regional Council, which have been adopted by Dundee City Council, residential homes for older people in Dundee meet an average of 92% of standards. The local authority's own homes, whilst meeting over 90% of standards in most areas, fall down in the standards applied to staffing, despite having high levels of frailty, particularly residents who are confused, in some of its homes. However, the local authority homes had the highest proportion of single rooms (100%), compared with 74% in the private sector and 89% in the voluntary sector.

12 Nursing homes in Dundee are caring for high levels of resident frailty. The quality of care was found by Tayside Health Board Inspectors to be generally good. However, one home had below registration standard staffing and high accident levels to residents.

Perth & Kinross

13 Perth & Kinross intend to develop their own standards by February 1997, and are at present consulting with providers about this. Their intention is to develop standards which will be "concise, realistic, but still....challenging and, most importantly, reflecting users' needs".

14 Before 1st April 1996 local authority homes in the area met the lowest average percentage of staffing standards. However, Perth & Kinross Council took early action to remedy the inadequacy of the inherited staffing levels in their residential homes. We welcome this step, with its immediate positive impact on the quality of care available to residents in these homes.

15 On the evidence available we concluded that independent sector homes in Perth & Kinross were meeting a higher percentage of standards than local authority homes. However the local authority has the best performance in relation to ensuring residents' privacy through the provision of single rooms. Had it been possible to include all the local authority and registered homes in the analysis, the performance levels may have been different.

16 Nursing home care is generally judged to be 'favourable' by Tayside Health Board inspectors, but one home was not providing good quality care. Since the nursing homes in Perth & Kinross are caring for high levels of physical and mental frailty, the fact that two homes are below registration levels on staffing gives cause for concern.

Value for money

We concluded that the costs of running the local authority homes are consistently in excess of the prices the authorities pay to purchase such care in the independent sector. We did not examine the relative costs of local authority, voluntary sector and private sector care. Some of the factors which contribute to the lower prices paid by local authorities for independent sector care are in fact additional costs to the public purse, though not to the local authorities. With the important exception of the provision of single rooms we did not find that the Councils' own homes generally provided a better standard of care. In Dundee City the local authority homes catered for more frail residents, but this was not the case in either Angus or Perth & Kinross. We concluded that there is scope for achieving good quality care at lower cost by making greater use of independent sector provision. We found that the major cost in providing residential care is staffing. The independent sector homes maintain as good or better staffing levels than the Council homes. We conclude therefore that they either operate at a loss (as we understand some of the voluntary sector homes do) or that they pay staff significantly less (as we understand the private sector homes do).

17 In the particular circumstances of this inspection, when all 3 departments have been required to make savings at the start of their operational life, close financial control has been uppermost in senior managers' minds. We were impressed by the budget scrutiny procedures and the close monitoring of residential and nursing home costs in each Council.

18 In considering value for money we examined the costs of community care services, alongside indicators about the frailty of service users and quality of care. Judgements as to value for money need to take these three factors into account and in developing local strategies the Councils also need to take account of the numbers of people and their range of needs. We concluded that each of the Councils should review its strategy for the provision and purchase of residential care services.

19 In our examination of value for money issues and potential savings, we looked closely at a number of factors which are likely to limit actual savings. We recognised that redeployment of staff or redundancies would each carry costs to the local authority, and we concluded that it is likely that new owners of former local authority homes would not be likely to accept the transfer of existing staff on protected wages and conditions. We also recognised that other factors, such as the need to increase the numbers of single rooms in the independent residential sector and a shift in the balance of public and privately-financed residential placements could lead to an increase in charges to local authorities.

20 We looked closely at what each each authority had to say in relation to the view that local authorities should remain direct providers of service. The Social Work (Scotland) Act 1968 does not simply impose a duty on local authorities to provide residential and other establishments. Section 59 states that "It shall be the duty of a local authority to provide and maintain such residential and other establishments as may be required for their functions under this Act, or arrange for the provision of such establishments." This clearly allows for an alternative to direct provision by the local authority.

21 In defending their higher costs, local authorities argue that taking good care of vulnerable older people is a complex task which requires competent staff, and which deserves to be appropriately rewarded. They say they pay their staff better rates than the

private sector, particularly those staff who work overtime, at weekends or in the evenings. In addition, they provide more formal training for their staff. Local authorities could encourage more formal training of independent sector staff, by allowing a sum of money, in any contract with the independent sector, specifically for training. Alternatively, they could allow independent sector staff to access their own local authority training programmes at marginal costs to themselves.

22 We accept that there is an argument for the local authority to remain as "provider of last resort", but conclude that this may not be absolute; independent sector providers could be contracted to deliver such services.

23 In reviewing their strategies for the delivery of community care services, local authorities must take due account of the capital costs of such provision, and must make sufficient resources available to allow for the rapid refurbishment of buildings or furnishings. The decision to close 2 local authority homes in Perth & Kinross was taken because the Council could not afford to bring these buildings up to the required standard. Furthermore, it was clear from our examination of the inspection reports submitted to us, that accommodation shortfalls were not always remedied speedily, often because of the capital expenditure involved. These issues will need to be considered carefully by local authorities when planning future services.

Angus

24 The weighted average cost of local authority residential care, at £431 per week (all residents) is considerably higher than the average price, £230, paid to the independent sector. Residential weighted average costs are higher than the standard published rate for Angus. Average Day Care costs at £31.45 per day are higher than the figure which is published in the Angus Community Care Action Plan. The average cost of Domiciliary Care should be recalculated, allowing an allocation of overheads.

25 Some individual local authority homes exceed weighted average costs by significant amounts.

26 On the evidence of our sample, a higher percentage of residents of nursing homes in Angus are likely to be "confused" or incontinent than people living in residential homes. The proportions of people who are bed or chairbound are very small in both types of provision. High levels of frailty occur much less in the one voluntary home in the sample. The frailty levels in local authority and private homes are similar, with one private home having a higher proportion of "confused" and incontinent residents than others in the sector. The highest proportions of "confusion" and incontinence are, nevertheless, in the nursing home sector.

27 Local authority homes in Angus did not meet as many of the present inspection standards as homes provided by the independent sector, although they did have the highest percentage of single rooms. Angus Council also acted swiftly to improve staffing levels in their own homes with effect from 1 April 1996 by reducing the number of beds. Since some local authority homes have high proportions of mentally frail residents, any shortfall in staffing levels is likely to have implications for the quality of care staff are able to give.

We conclude that:

the cost to Angus Council of directly running its own homes is in excess of prices paid to independent sector providers for equivalent care,

these costs do not reflect provision for a more frail population, or a better quality of care, and therefore

Angus Council should urgently review its strategies for the provision and purchase of residential care services for older people.

Dundee

28 The weighted average cost of local authority residential care, at £313 per week, is higher than the average price, £217, paid to the independent sector, but within the Council's published rate. The actual weighted average cost of local authority day care services is above the figure published in the Dundee Community Care Action Plan. More work needs to be done locally to establish the actual cost of domiciliary care services, which is presently calculated as £6.16 per hour.

29 Dundee City Council has closed one local authority home in 1996. This decision was driven, in part, by a need for financial savings. We comment further on this later, in our conclusions on the planning, provision and purchasing of services. We have concluded that Dundee City Council, facing a need to identify further savings, has scope for achieving good quality care by making greater use of independent providers.

30 On the basis of the information available to us, most of the frailest older people living in residential or nursing home care in Dundee are either in local authority residential homes or are in nursing homes. On the whole, the independent sector residential homes in our sample are not coping with high levels of frailty. Nursing homes have the highest proportions of "confused" and incontinent residents, but Dundee has a large number of local authority homes, and some of these homes have high levels of residents who are "confused" or incontinent or both.

31 Using the standards and indicators developed by Dundee City Council, residential homes for older people in Dundee meet an average of 92% of standards. The local authority's own homes, whilst meeting over 90% of standards in most areas, fall down in the standards applied to staffing, despite having high levels of frailty in some of its homes. Voluntary homes have the highest overall average percentage of standards met by the independent sector homes. We have commented earlier on the relative proportions of single rooms across the sectors.

We conclude that:

the cost to Dundee City Council of directly running its own homes is in excess of prices paid to independent sector providers for equivalent care,

these costs may reflect provision for a more frail population, but do not reflect a better quality of care and do not reflect higher staffing levels, and therefore

Dundee City Council should urgently review its strategies for the provision and purchase of residential care services for older people.

Perth & Kinross

32 The average cost of local authority residential care, at £375 per week, is significantly higher than the average price, £224, paid to the independent sector. The cost is higher than the standard published rate. Average Day Care costs at £29.83 per day, are higher than the figure which is published in the Perth & Kinross Community Care Action Plan. Average Domiciliary Care costs are £6.32 per hour,

33 Nursing homes in Perth & Kinross appear to be accommodating the most frail residents, particularly those who are "confused". Two private homes in our sample do not have any residents meeting any of our three frailty criteria. On the other hand, some private homes record higher levels of "confusion" amongst residents than occur in either the local authority or voluntary sector homes.

34 On the evidence available we conclude that independent sector homes in Perth & Kinross met a higher percentage of standards than were met by authority homes. However the local authority has the best performance in relation to ensuring residents' privacy through the provision of single rooms. Perth & Kinross Council has sold two of its homes to the private sector in the present year. We comment further on this later, in our conclusions relating to the planning, provision and purchasing of services.

We conclude that:

the cost to Perth & Kinross Council of directly running its own homes is in excess of prices paid to independent sector providers for equivalent care,

these costs do not reflect provision for a more frail population, a better quality of care or higher staffing levels, and therefore

Perth & Kinross Council should urgently review its strategies for the provision and purchase of residential care services for older people.

The planning, provision and purchasing of services

We conclude that provision of services was not sufficiently matched to need; that service planning across the three council areas required significant improvement; that purchasing intentions need to be clearly stated and that there needed to be stronger alignment between service and financial planning. We consider that each of the Councils should extend their experience in commissioning and purchasing residential care to include day, domiciliary and respite care.

35 There are several means of undertaking an assessment of population needs; we published guidance on this earlier in 1996 which should assist authorities in the future. In this inspection we have applied one model, Isaacs' framework for Intervals of Need, to the population of older people 75+ in each Council area. We sought to relate that analysis of need to existing levels of provision. This analysis, undertaken within a short period of time, indicated that the provision of services in the 3 authorities is not well matched to the needs of older people.

36 Our own analysis is not exhaustive. Nor would we seek to defend some of the detail within that analysis. We do consider that such an analysis, or a similar exercise, is a necessary precursor to detailed planning and purchase of services.

37 We found in all 3 Councils that the 1996-97 community care plan failed to meet the requirements of the Direction on Purchasing[30]. In our view clarity about purchasing intentions is necessary to avoid placing provider businesses at risk and discouraging new providers from entering what they perceive to be a risk market.

38 The arrangements for the purchasing of community care services are central to the reforms introduced in April 1993. They are central to the development of flexible provision, to the choices available to service users and to issues of value for money. They are likely to have become more important with local government reorganisation. The Accounts Commission[31], anticipating that there would be a substantial increase in the number of social work authorities, suggested that those authorities which are relatively small in size would be unable to directly provide the full range of specialist services required and would need to commission and purchase services from other providers.

39 We found few links between service and financial planning. The community care planning and budget cycles of each council occur at different times in the year. At present the budget cycle precedes that of service planning. The costs of service developments are, therefore, provided within, rather than contribute to, the budget cycle.

40 A local authority's central task is to secure those services which it has identified are required. Local authorities have been encouraged to adopt the role of enablers and to purchase the most appropriate services, regardless of which sector provides them, to meet individuals' assessed needs and choices in a cost-effective way. Authorities should not only purchase those services which are already available but should encourage new developments. The authority should specify the standards for those services and purchase them from within the "mixed economy of care".

41 We found all 3 Councils had substantial experience of commissioning and purchasing, both in-house and from the independent sector.

Angus

42 We concluded that the balance of care provision in Angus is at present weighted heavily towards hospital care. There is sufficient residential and nursing home provision, but less day care provision than appears to be required. Home help provision is currently available to most service users on one or 2 days each week, and our estimates of the numbers of people with need for intensive support suggest the current service does not contribute significantly to the care of the more frail older population. We conclude that the Council needs to develop more flexible and responsive domiciliary care services.

43 The absence of quantifiable targets and specified volumes of services in the current Community Care Action Plan limit the extent to which it may be used by the department to monitor progress towards agreed objectives. Angus Council state that these matters will be addressed in the new Community Care Plan for 1997-2000.

44 At present there is not a sufficiently close alignment between service and financial planning. We considered that the new planning arrangements being put in place provide an opportunity for all key interest groups to express their views and to plan effectively. The development of the Angus Mental Health Strategy is a welcome model for the development of future service strategies, such as the strategy for older people.

45 On purchasing we welcome the new initiatives to purchase elements of domiciliary care from the voluntary sector. Angus already purchases much of its day care provision from voluntary organisations. We have been informed that Angus Council, at present, has no intention of purchasing domiciliary care from the private sector. The Director outlined broad plans for the development of the Council's residential homes into resource centres, providing day and home care to the areas in which the homes are situated. We were not convinced that this was a realisable strategy and consider that a more immediate review of how to make detailed cost-effective improvements to the current mix of provision is required.

46 We found no evidence of bias or discrimination against the use of independent sector residential or nursing homes in Angus.

47 We believe that it would assist the local authority to make informed decisions about purchasing nursing home care if Tayside Health Board could make inspection reports on nursing homes available to them.

48 The introduction of charges for widely-used services which were hitherto free will always be a difficult exercise. We were pleased to learn that the council will be monitoring the impact of the charges on a quarterly basis, although the monitoring described to us seemed to be largely financial. It was not clear to us whether information on the numbers of users declining services would be made available, nor whether there would be any attempt to evaluate the impact on people who paid for services but were only just over the payment liability level set by the local authority.

Dundee

49 Dundee has relatively few older people requiring intensive support in continuing care beds in local hospitals. The greater number of such people are accommodated in residential (largely local authority) and nursing homes. The home help service is targeted on meeting the largely practical needs of service users, once or twice a week. We conclude that there is a need to develop more flexible and responsive domiciliary care services. Dundee City provides a particularly high level of sheltered housing, which is an important factor in the council's approach to the provision of services to older people, and potentially its major asset in providing high quality home care for those older people requiring daily support.

50 The local authority recently closed one of its residential homes. As we have noted earlier, such a change can present very difficult problems for older people who are required to make a further move from "their home". Dundee City Council managed this complex and sensitive task well, and we commend them on their achievement.

51 The current Community Care Plan is insufficiently detailed to enable it to be used as an effective management tool for monitoring progress towards agreed objectives and

targets. In our view this is the primary purpose of such plans. It is important to improve the linkages between the financial and strategic planning processes, which currently operate to different timeframes.

52 Dundee City Council is reviewing its policy on purchasing community care services. It has purchased services from voluntary organisations since its inception but has not hitherto purchased private sector domiciliary or day care.

53 We found no evidence of bias or discrimination against the use of independent sector residential or nursing homes in Dundee City.

54 We believe it would assist the local authority to make informed decisions about purchasing nursing home care if Tayside Health Board could make inspection reports on nursing homes available to them.

55 Since 1 April 1996, Dundee also has made significant use of private sector nursing homes. Vacancy levels in nursing homes in Dundee are high, but this is because the number of beds has increased well in excess of anticipated increases in the number of admissions.

56 The introduction of charges for non-residential services was inevitably difficult and unpopular despite the sensitive and careful approach with which the Council proceeded. Plans are in hand to monitor the impact on the uptake of services.

Perth & Kinross

57 Community care services for people requiring intensive support in Perth & Kinross are focused particularly on residential and nursing home care. The home help service continues to be geared towards meeting the mainly practical needs of older people, and is not as yet targeted on meeting the needs of the more frail older population. We conclude that the Council needs to develop more flexible and responsive domiliary care services.

58 In an important development the local authority recently sold two of their residential care homes to the private sector. As we have noted earlier, such a change can present very difficult problems for older people who are required to make a further move from "their home". Perth & Kinross managed this complex and sensitive process well, and we commend them on their achievement.

59 The absence of quantifiable targets and specified volumes of services in the current Community Care Action Plan limit the extent to which it may be used by the department to monitor progress towards agreed objectives. The local authority has now established a planning framework which reflects closely the guidance issued by SWSG, and which seems likely to generate a greater degree of ownership of the Plan than has been the case to date. There is already evidence that the new arrangements are working effectively. The Council has made a positive start to the development of their 1997-2000 Community Care Plan, an early Draft of which has been well received by the private sector.

60 On purchasing, Perth & Kinross has demonstrated a pragmatic approach to working with the independent sector, with regard to residential care. That approach has the potential for being replicated with day and domiciliary care. The manner in which the

community care budget is devolved to community care teams should facilitate wider purchasing activity by local managers.

61 We found no evidence of bias or discrimination against the use of independent sector residential or nursing homes in Perth & Kinross.

62 In our view it would assist the local authority to reach informed decisions about purchasing nursing home care if Tayside Health Board could make reports on nursing homes available to them.

63 The introduction of charges for domiciliary care services inevitably presented the council with administrative and logistical problems, as well as critical comment from some quarters. The local authority has worked hard to resolve the initial billing problems, and has taken a number of steps to address the reasonable concerns of service users who are assessed as being liable to pay for the services they receive. We hope these steps will prove successful.

Information

We concluded that lack of information was a crucial factor effectively limiting the successful implementation of community care at a number of different levels across all 3 Council areas.

The provision of information to service users

64 The needs of older people should be the primary consideration for all service providers and great care should be taken to ensure they are as informed as possible about whatever choices are available to them. In particular, a move to residential care is a major decision which older people should only be asked to make once in their lives. It is vital that it is the right decision and a careful assessment of individual needs should be complemented by the provision of clear information about possible choices and any associated service charges so that older people and their carers are as fully informed as possible.

65 In addition once older people have moved into care they should be fully informed about their rights and it is important that their involvement is sought in planning that care.

Angus

66 Only half of those people in residential or nursing home care in our sample of users had been given a range of homes from which to make a choice. A few people had already selected the home to which they wished to move before social workers or care managers became involved. The proportion of people who were made aware of the possibility of "topping-up" independent sector care costs was relatively small (less than a third) and there was some evidence that some self-paying residents in local authority homes had not been made aware of this possibility, despite their feeling that the costs of care were very important. All the people interviewed in private care or in nursing homes were paying all or part of the charges themselves and unsurprisingly saw charges as important or very important.

67 From the interviews with the sample of 10 people receiving support to live at home, we concluded that people were only offered a choice of the services to be provided, not about which agency would provide the service. Even this degree of choice was only made available to a minority of those interviewed. Just over half those interviewed were paying for services, and two-thirds of this group attached little importance to costs. Most of the people were living alone , but most also had the additional support of family carers which contributed to them being able to continue living at home despite considerable levels of frailty.

68 We concluded that, in Angus, social work practice in making information and choices available to service users is uneven.

69 The revised information leaflet issued by Angus Council about the introduction of charges for non-residential care services, does not advise service users that they may make representations against their assessed liability.

70 Residents in Angus homes, whatever the sector, were not fully involved in their care planning. There was evidence in inspection reports that although residents may have signed their contracts with the homes that they were unaware what they had signed, did not know their rights in respect of the contract and were not in possession of it.

Dundee

71 Only half of the people in our sample who had moved into long-stay care had been offered a range of care homes across sectors from which to make a choice. The majority of carers in our sample had not been informed about charges for care, despite considering them to be important. In our sample, a minority of people living in very sheltered housing had been given a choice of possible services but none had been given a choice of provider. Most people had not been given information about the charging policy, although two-thirds of them were paying for services. Most thought that the charges were unimportant. A minority of tenants had learnt about very sheltered housing as a solution to their difficulties after first contemplating or trying out residential or nursing home care and finding it unsatisfactory. Very sheltered housing has the potential to be a very satisfactory solution for people with high care needs but who wish to retain a high degree of autonomy.

72 Half of the people receiving domiciliary care services at home had been offered a choice of service but very few had also been offered a choice of provider. Although almost all the domiciliary users were paying for their community care services, only a minority remembered receiving information about charges. Only a minority, however, thought charges were important.

73 We concluded that, in Dundee, social work practice in making information and choices available to service users is uneven.

74 When Dundee City Council introduced charges for non-residential services it was not clear whether users were also advised that they could make representations against their assessed liability for charges.

75 In addition homes across all sectors in Dundee did not fully involve residents in their care planning.

Perth & Kinross

76 We concluded that less than half the people who had moved into long-stay residential or nursing home care in Perth & Kinross had been given a choice of homes. A smaller proportion of people had been informed about the possibility of "topping-up" the costs of independent sector homes which charge above the local approved rate. It is possible that failure to make this information more widely available limited people's choices, perhaps unnecessarily. None of the residential sample of people interviewed had thought charges to be important in their decision-making.

77 The people living in very sheltered housing who had been offered choices about services were also a minority. Two-thirds of this group of people were paying for services, but very few could recall being given information about the basis on which the charges were levied. Half of the domiciliary care users in Perth & Kinross had been given a choice of services but not of service provider. The same proportion of users had been informed about the basis on which charges were levied and thought charges had been important or very important in their decision-making.

78 We concluded that, in Perth & Kinross, social work practice in relation to making information and choices available to service users is uneven.

79 When Perth & Kinross introduced charges for non-residential services the information they issued informed users of the Director of Social Work's power to reduce or waive charges in certain circumstances.

80 Local authority homes sampled in the inspection did not fully involve residents of these homes in all aspects of their care planning.

The provision of information to staff involved in assessment and to service managers

81 Two years ago the Accounts Commission[32] reported on the information deficits within local authorities, 18 months after community care had been introduced. The Commission identified 3 specific deficiencies; information gaps, poor integration of different datasets and under-utilisation of existing data. We found that these deficiencies continued within all 3 authorities of Angus, Dundee and Perth & Kinross.

82 Information gaps impact upon the working lives of both operational staff and managers. The absence of readily available and detailed information about unit costs means that staff carrying out assessments of need are unlikely to be clear about what choice would represent, for example, best value for money. For managers, planning and then developing services requires accurate financial information about current budgets.

83 The 3 authorities of Angus, Dundee and Perth & Kinross all state they are committed to taking forward jointly the computerised client and service information package (K2). Work was started by the former Tayside Region but we found the software package remains in an early stage of development. We were shown, for example, the training suite for staff at Perth & Kinross, the Training Plan and overall Office Information Systems plan. The Perth & Kinross target is to train over 200 staff in using the system in 1996-97.

84 The integration of different datasets is also some way off. Client and service information have not yet been linked with financial information held on INTEGRA, the corporate finance department's software. Information managers in each of the authorities indicated that integration was, for operational purposes, several years away. Delays in coding arrangements, a by-product of local government reorganisation, have impeded moves towards integration further.

85 There was evidence too that authorities were not using existing data as fully as they might. Our own approach to this inspection, using existing data, allowed the development of a "map" of both needs and provision in relation to older people. There was little evidence that such a map, an indicator for planning purposes, had been developed within the 3 authorities. A second example is the development of aggregate assessment of needs from data held about individuals. There were few examples of the authorities drawing on the individual assessments of service users to project the range and pattern of service requirements.

86 As the Accounts Commission have indicated[33] information is central to making community care work. Angus, Dundee and Perth & Kinross are not alone in the relatively limited progress made towards the development of effective management information systems. Nor are they alone in having invested substantial capital sums to enhance and develop such systems. Between 1991-95 over £6m has been spent by local authorities throughout Scotland to this end.

87 The Accounts Commission made a strong case for sharing experiences of the development of information systems to support community care. This process was started with a joint COSLA/Scottish Office Standing Group on Community Care Information Requirements. The Standing Group, which has not met since reorganisation, recommended that a study of information systems should be undertaken. That study has not yet taken place.

The provision of information to and communication with private providers

88 Private sector providers have consistently expressed concern about a number of issues already addressed in this report. They have complained about a lack of information from, and poor communication with, the respective authorities. In particular, there was a widespread view amongst providers that local authorities were insufficiently clear and open about their purchasing intentions.

89 This lack of clarity about purchasing intentions has been addressed by us earlier, but it is clear that without such a sharing of information about purchasing intentions many providers felt unable to make any firm plans for future business developments. In their turn, providers need to recognise that the budgetary constraints under which local authorities may be operating will inevitably impact on their policies and practice. We agree with a view expressed recently by the Nuffield Institute for Health that local authorities should develop mature purchasing arrangements involving long-term relationships with providers[34] whom they consider provide good quality and cost-effective care. These relationships should be based on mutual support and a shared understanding of each other's motivations, intentions and requirements. There should, after all, be a common objective in meeting the needs of older people.

90 There is some evidence to suggest that the emergence of the new authorities will contribute to establishing improved communication. This already appears to be the case in Perth & Kinross.

COMMENTS BY LAY MEMBER

The Inspection was assisted by Ms Anja Amsel who was recommended to us as a lay member of the Inspection Team by Age Concern Scotland. We have involved lay people (i.e. people who are not professional social workers or employed in the agencies being inspected) in all our inspections since 1993.

Anja Amsel brought a unique perspective to our work. She has previously worked extensively in the Housing field, particularly with Housing Associations , and she is currently involved in a variety of voluntary activities.

"I have welcomed the opportunity to participate as a Lay Inspector in the team carrying out this piece of work. I was very well briefed and supported by the officers from the Social Work Services Inspectorate, from whom I learned much about the whole system and the role and functions of the Inspectorate generally.

I participated in the fieldwork, interviewing users of the service in very sheltered housing scheme and also meeting the purchasers and providers of the service. I participated in a meeting where the views of the private sector providers were expounded at some length. I also assisted in the analysis of the Social Work Inspection Reports.

This, together with my reading has given me an overview of how the system might work. I did not however have time or scope to look at the role of carers.

I concur overall with the findings of the report. However participation in the process and my own background as a special needs housing provider, from a national voluntary organisation, have generated some additional comments.

In its most basic form, need generates provision, but there is a limited amount of provision to meet needs.

What did not appear to be demonstrated adequately, even taking into account the separate Community Care and Action Plans was an overview or strategic approach to the whole process, looking at issues of present and future needs. Consequently considerable competition is generated, both between public, voluntary and private sectors. The corporate providers have not yet moved into the arena, but it is likely that this may yet become another competitive element.

Additionally, both the Community Care Plans and Action Plans, for all three authorities, lacked basic financial information. In a climate of scare resources this makes it difficult fully to evaluate them.

The market mapping has shown the disparity of provision both in terms of over supply and unmet needs. This was demonstrated in the unevenness of provision particularly for people with critical and short Intervals of Need (cf. Appendix I). In discussing this whole area account must be taken of the different geographical terrain within the three authorities: for example Perth & Kinross is one of the largest rural areas in Scotland, whereas Dundee is urban. This will obviously affect the size and the nature of services in residential or nursing homes, or own homes, where domiciliary care is an issue.

It does seem that some more integration might be possible between the different providers and social work, health board and housing agencies. Presumably the new authorities require time to develop these aspects.

As far as charging policies are concerned, discrepancies were identified. This is a difficult issue because of the hidden costs. The concept of charging cannot be seen purely in local authority cost terms, since the total claim on the public purse should be taken into account when making assessments (housing benefit, income support, disparate old age pensions).

Value for money is an important issue both in physical and in qualitative terms. We were asked to evaluate the services and this matter is addressed in the main report. Broad questions arise however, some of which might prove to be outwith the terms of this review. For example, is there a disparity in the level of charges in the private sector and if so, what criteria do the local authorities have in purchasing? If there are disparities are they due to the quality of provision? By what criteria do the private sector set their charges?

Such questions raise also the issues of consumer choice. Among the residents that I interviewed (in a high quality housing association scheme), their choice had been made on the basis of the reputation of the scheme, gained through neighbour and family networks. It became clear overall however that users had not been made aware of choice alternatives when selecting a home.

There was little resentment on the part of users to the cost of services: as an example the companionship provided by the home helps and a walker/attendant for a blind person were important factors.

Charging therefore, as an issue was of less concern than the fact of paying for accommodation itself, which people felt should be theirs by right. This view was very widely expressed.

The key issue in providing care is a moral/philosophical one; namely the belief of the older generation, of leaving something to their children, is widely held. And in this context the home is the lodestar. Yet the view now is that the value of a home is a major asset and is needed by the system to provide care for the frail elderly. There is a dilemma here: health care (also important to the elderly) is free at the point of delivery, but social care is means tested and must be paid for. This continues to be one of the key issues that bedevils the value for money argument and users of the service appear well aware of it.

In terms of assessing the quality of life of residents, the inspection visits and reports are an important function. What did appear to emerge from this, particularly in the private sector was that residents were not adequately informed about or aware of their contractual rights or choices. Nor did they always appear to know about a system of complaints procedure. It could abate any unease about charges if this issue were more open.

Inspection reports did also on occasion identify design faults important in structural or safety terms. The time scale given to remedy these was sometimes up to three years (probably beyond the life expectancy of present residents). A greater sense of urgency in responding to matters raised in the inspection reports would sometimes appear to be indicated.

It is important to know what is the policy of the local authorities in providing their own facilities as against purchasing. This is a major factor in evaluating the efficiency of the services delivered to clients in either the public, voluntary or private sectors.

Furthermore a most fundamental question arises in this context: who represents the client? Customer satisfaction must be the key issue and residential services must include a measure of choice, so that they meet the criteria of independence, privacy and dignity. These are essential aims which could become buried in the value for money argument.

It does appear somewhat as if the needs and wishes of the individual clients become submerged in the general administrative machinery. Indeed, there appeared an over-emphasis on the administrative aspects of standards of care, rather than on the provision of life enhancement and varied experiences.

I felt that my role in this inspection was to understand the issues, gain an overview of the mechanics of the whole process and finally to concentrate on the services to users. And given that there is an inexorable rise in the population of the elderly, there will be ever more people coming into the dependent category, calling upon the gamut of community care services.

I have been highly interested in having participated in this review. As a lay inspector it is possible to ask quite basic questions and to expect to find answers/resolutions. From my own professional background I comprehend the relationships between officers and members on local authorities and how this might bear upon policies. I am also aware of the constraints under which local authority officers have to operate. Both of these factors certainly appear to impinge upon the system.

Within the delivery of care in the community services to frail elderly in the three local authorities, there are undeniably tensions. I doubt whether this affects the quality of service delivered – this appeared of a high and caring order – but it may have affected opportunities for choice. "

Anja Amsel

RECOMMENDATIONS FOR ANGUS COUNCIL

1 Angus Council should review its draft quality service standards for residential homes to encourage greater focus on the aspirations and wishes of older people who move into residential care.

2 The Council should also take account of older people's aspirations and wishes when it reviews its registration and inspection standards. Individual standards should be weighted and reduced in number.

3 Angus Council should pursue its current negotiations with Tayside Health Board to secure joint work between the local authority and the Board on inspection.

4 Angus Council should continue to shift the balance of care for those older people requiring intensive support from hospital and nursing home provision to community-based provision. This changing balance should, with Health Board support, include domicilary care developments that address the needs of those older people who require frequent and skilled support.

5 Angus Council should review its' approach to community care planning to ensure the 1997-2000 plans become more purposeful documents. In particular, the Council should:

link aggregate need to service provision and identify service gaps and deficiencies;

include specific and measurable objectives;

match specific financial commitments to service developments;

comply with the Government's Directions on Purchasing by including a clear statement of purchasing intentions which estimates the volume of services required and expenditure estimates by sector.

6 Angus Council should take steps to align its strategic and financial planning cycles.

7 Angus Council should review the implications of the differing costs of its own residential services against the prices paid to the independent sector. The review should consider the role and need for local authority direct provision taking into account issues of quality, volume demand and cost. The Council should review its approach to contract specification to ensure it includes staff training and other appropriate requirements. The review should inform the Councils' purchasing intentions over the next 5 years.

8 The unit costs of the Council's community care services should be publicly available, and where such costs are higher than in the independent sector the authority should clearly state the value added quality these costs secure.

9 Angus Council should amend its published standard rate for residential care by December 1996. Angus Council should ensure that it follows the CIPFA/COSLA guidance in allowing for capital charges to be included in the standard rates.

10 Angus Council should examine the scope for purchasing quality domiciliary, day and respite care services from the private sector, where such services can be provided at a competitive cost.

11 Angus Council should improve its information to service users about services and associated charges. The Council needs to make clear to service users that they can make representations against their assessed liability for non-residential care service charges. Residents in care should be fully informed about their rights and involved in planning individual aspects of their care.

12 Angus Council should monitor the impact of the introduction of charging policies for home care through an examination of all cases where existing services were cancelled by users, following these up by letter and personal contact. The Council should analyse service take-up/rejection rates by people newly assessed as requiring the service.

13 Angus Council should take steps to improve the current level of management information available at unit or cost centre level. Subject to satisfactory systems of financial control, they should devolve purchasing budgets to care managers by April 1998.

14 Angus Council should establish regular formal meetings with representatives of independent providers, by the end of December 1996, to help achieve the common objective of best meeting the needs of older people.

RECOMMENDATIONS FOR DUNDEE CITY COUNCIL

1 Dundee City Council should review its registration and inspection standards for residential homes to encourage greater focus on the aspirations and wishes of older people who move into residential care. Individual standards should be weighted and reduced in number.

2 Dundee City Council should consolidate social care for older people requiring intensive support within the community through the development of its domiciliary care services. Older people who need intensive support should be the focus of its joint strategy with Tayside Health Board.

3 Dundee City Council should review its approach to community care planning to ensure the 1997-2000 plans become purposeful documents. In particular, the Council should:

> link aggregate need to service provision, and identify service gaps and deficiencies;
>
> include specific and measurable objectives;
>
> match specific financial commitments to service developments;
>
> comply with the Government's Directions on Purchasing by including a clear statement of purchasing intentions which estimates the volume of services required and expenditure estimates by sector.

4 Dundee City Council should take steps to align its strategic and financial planning cycles.

5 Dundee City Council should review the implications of the differing costs of its own residential care services against the prices paid to the independent sector. The review should consider the role and need for local authority direct provision taking into account issues of quality, volume demand and cost. The Council should review its approach to contract specification to ensure it includes staff training and other appropriate requirements. The review should inform the Councils' purchasing intentions over the next 5 years.

6 The unit costs of the Council's community care services should be publicly available, and where such costs are higher than in the independent sector the authority should clearly state the added value these costs secure.

7 Dundee City Council should examine the scope for purchasing quality domiciliary, day and respite care services from the private sector, where such services can be provided at a competitive cost.

8 Dundee City Council should improve its information to service users about services and associated charges. The Council needs to make clear to service users that they can make representations against assessed liability. Residents in care should be fully informed about their rights and involved in planning individual aspects of their care.

9 Dundee City Council should take steps to improve the current level of management information available at unit or cost centre level. Subject to satisfactory systems of financial control, they should devolve purchasing budgets to care managers by April 1998.

10 Dundee City Council should establish regular formal meetings with representatives of independent providers, by the end of December 1996, to help achieve the common objective of best meeting the needs of older people.

RECOMMENDATIONS FOR PERTH & KINROSS COUNCIL

1 Perth & Kinross Council should ensure that its revised registration and inspection standards reflect the aspirations and wishes of older people who move into residential care.

2 Perth & Kinross Council should seek to collaborate more closely with Tayside Health Board in standard-setting and inspection of residential and nursing homes.

3 Perth & Kinross Council should continue to shift the balance of care for those older people requiring intensive support from hospital and nursing home provision to community-based provision. This changing balance should, with Health Board support, include domicilary care developments that address the needs of older people who require frequent and skilled support.

4 Perth & Kinross Council should review its approach to community care planning to ensure the 1997-2000 plans become purposeful documents. In particular, the Council should:

link aggregate need to service provision, and identify service gaps and deficiencies;

include specific and measurable objectives;

match specific financial commitments to service developments.

comply with the Government's Directions on Purchasing by including a clear statement of purchasing intentions which estimates the volume of services required and expenditure estimates by sector.

5 Perth & Kinross Council should take steps to align its strategic and financial planning cycles.

6 Perth & Kinross Council should review the implications of the differing costs of its own residential services against the prices paid to the independent sector. The review should consider the role and need for local authority direct provision taking into account issues of quality, volume demand and cost. The Council should review its approach to contract specification to ensure it includes staff training and other appropriate requirements. The review should inform the Councils' purchasing intentions over the next 5 years.

7 The unit costs of the Council's community care services should be publicly available, and where such costs are higher than in the independent sector the authority should state clearly the value added quality these costs secure.

8 Perth & Kinross Council should amend its published standard rate for residential care by December 1996.

9 Perth & Kinross Council should examine the scope for purchasing quality domiciliary, day and respite care services from the private sector, where such care can be provided at a competitive cost.

10 Perth & Kinross Council should improve its information to service users about services and associated charges. Residents in care should be fully informed about their rights and involved in planning individual aspects of their care.

11 Perth & Kinross Council should take steps to improve the current level of management information available at unit or cost centre level. Subject to satisfactory systems of financial control, they should devolve purchasing budgets to care managers by April 1998.

12 Perth & Kinross Council should establish regular formal meetings with representatives of independent providers, by the end of December 1996, to help achieve the common objective of best meeting the needs of older people.

RECOMMENDATION FOR TAYSIDE HEALTH BOARD

1 The Health Board should make final inspection reports of nursing homes available to inspection units and purchasing managers of all 3 Councils.

RECOMMENDATIONS FOR THE SCOTTISH OFFICE

1 The Scottish Office should commission the production of a good practice guide for local authorities on how best to provide information to older people about services and associated charges.

2 The Scottish Office should review with COSLA by April 1997 the role and work of the Standing Group on Community Care Information Requirements, with a view to identifying information about good practice in management information systems and disseminating this across Scotland.

3 The Scottish Office should review the progress made by Angus, Dundee City and Perth & Kinross Councils in developing community care services. In particular, it should review the progress of resource transfer from Tayside Health Board to Perth & Kinross Council, and the effectiveness of each Council's arrangements for formal meetings with independent providers.

Appendix I

Matching The Needs of, And Provision for, Older People Aged 75+

We estimated the differing needs of frail older people using Isaacs' model of Intervals of Need. We explain how current data about provision of services may be considered in relation to Intervals of Need. Finally we explain how we have reached our judgements about whether services match the needs of older people, 75+.

1. Intervals of need

The key aspect of Isaacs' model is that he identifies at what intervals a person may require assistance. In other words, needs are conceptualised as a function of time rather than of a particular disability, or of a particular age. Isaacs identifies 3 main 'intervals' of need, namely Critical, Short and Long. These are defined in the table below.

Isaacs' model for assessing intervals of needs includes specific indicators for each interval. These individual indicators allow the number of older people 75+ with particular needs, in any given population, to be calculated. The calculation can be undertaken by applying widely available prevalence data. Using this model some multi-disabled people may be counted more than once. The final figures are, therefore, only indicative.

One major source of such data, albeit based on UK wide rather than solely Scottish populations, is the General Household Survey (GHS)[35]. The Survey provides estimates of older people living in private households, with needs for assistance that relate closely to Isaacs' specific indicators.

The GHS Survey does not include information about the numbers of people in communal establishments (residential homes, nursing homes and hospitals) who may require assistance. It is necessary therefore to calculate such numbers and add them to those living in private households. In this exercise we have used information about residents of residential and nursing homes taken from SWSG and Information and Statistics Division information which is regularly collected as a matter of routine from local authorities, independent agencies and health agencies.

Table 1 below provides a graphical explanation of this model, and the uses to which it may be put. The left hand column defines the 3 intervals, the middle column provides indicators for each Interval of Need, the right hand column indicates the prevalence rates used by SWSI.

Table 1 Applying prevalence rates to Isaacs' intervals of need

Isaacs' Classification	Specific Indicators	Prevalence source
"CRITICAL INTERVAL"		
The person needs assistance throughout the day and night, with unexpected, unpredictable frequency.	1. Inability to rise from bed or chair, walk to the toilet unassisted	1. Table 31, GHS, Unable to manage getting in and out of bed + Table 2.14 SWSG Bulletin (Disabilities of residents in homes for older people) + Table 6d-2 ISD (NHS) Disabilities of residents in nursing homes)
	2. Incontinence of urine or faeces	2. Campbell et al + Table 2.14 SWSG + Table 6d-2 ISD
	3. Mental "abnormality". (Dementia is the current term)	3. Jorm, Korten and Henderson
"SHORT INTERVAL"		
The person needs assistance every few hours by day, at predictable intervals	Unable to prepare or consume a meal, dress or undress	Table 45 Unable to cook a main meal by themselves
"LONG INTERVAL"		
The person needs assistance once in 24 hours or less often	Unable to perform one or more tasks	Table 47 Needing help in at least one domestic care task

The GHS tables provide information about these characteristics with reference to all older people and older people living alone. Whether an older person lives alone is a key indicator of whether formal support may be required.

Not all older people needing assistance, say, with one or more domestic tasks require formal support. Nevertheless the number of all older people who do require such assistance can be said to represent an upper range of the numbers who may do. That is the maximum number of people for whom formal provision of assistance is required.

The number of older people who do live alone in mainstream housing (or who live in a communal establishment) and who require assistance with activities of daily living represents the lower range of the numbers who are estimated to require formal assistance. That is the minimum number of people for whom the provision of assistance is required.

The Table below indicates an application of this method to the 75+ populations in Angus, Dundee and Perth & Kinross. There are some detailed notes about the individual calculations used at the end of this Appendix. They are to be read in conjunction with the attached spreadsheet.

Table 1.1 Estimated numbers people 75+, with Critical, Short and Long Intervals of Need.

Angus

Interval	Upper range		Lower range	
Critical (bed bound)	612		531	
Critical (incontinence)	1061		517	
Critical (dementia)	926		483	
Critical (total)		2599		1531
Short		891		224
Long		2189		1022

Dundee

Interval	Upper range		Lower range	
Critical (bed bound)	866		766	
Critical (incontinence)	1345		906	
Critical (dementia)	1141		595	
Critical (total)		3352		2267
Short		1098		416
Long		2696		1901

Perth & Kinross

Interval	Upper range		Lower range	
Critical (bed bound)	994		866	
Critical (incontinence)	1412		760	
Critical (dementia)	1169		610	
Critical (total)		3575		2236
Short		1125		303
Long		2761		1384

2. Data on the provision of services

The data on the levels of service provision is derived from the 1996/97 Community Care Plans of each authority. We have organised that data into 3 broad groupings. The groupings include services by the frequency (or intervals) at which assistance is assumed to be given. Group 1 includes those services that provide the most intensive support, Group 3 the least intensive. In making the judgement about whether service provision matches needs we have compared Group 1 services with Critical Intervals of Need, Group 2 with Short Intervals and Group 3 with Long Intervals.

Group 1

These are services that provide intensive support, i.e. they can meet the needs of people who require a great deal of support – Isaacs' "critical interval" people – namely day and night, and at frequent and unpredictable intervals. These include:

- hospital beds
- beds in residential homes, nursing homes and very sheltered housing
- support from a social care officer, and
- home help 6/7 days a week

Group 2

These are services that provide regular support, i.e. they can support people who need help at predictable intervals, several times a day – Isaacs' "short interval" people.

- sheltered housing
- day centres
- district nurses (and the number of visits per person)
- home help 3/4/5 days each week
- meals on wheels
- community alarms
- Crossroads Care attendants

Group 3

These are services which are typically available once a day, or less, i.e. they can meet the needs of people who need help once a day or less – Isaacs' "long interval" people. They are essentially practical or domestic services. These include:

- home help 1/2 days each week
- aids to daily living, e.g. occupational therapy aids..

3. Matching needs to provision

The judgement about whether provision matches estimated needs requires the levels of service provision and the level of individual needs to be expressed in the same language. This is achieved, in this model, by looking at the amount of service provided per 1,000 population of people 75+ and the incidence of need for help in the population of people aged 75 and over reported by the GHS.

We have taken the numbers of people 75+ in each authority, and grouped them by Intervals of Need. These have been expressed as a rate per 1,000 of the 75+ population. The source of these rates is the population of each authority (75+) and Table 1.1 Estimated numbers people 75+, with Critical, Short and Long Intervals of Need.

Next we have expressed the levels of service provision, within the 3 Groupings described above, in terms of rates of provision per 1,000 population of people 75+. As an illustration we have used the matching task with relation to older people with critical intervals of need in Angus.

Table 1.2 Needs of and provision for people aged 75+ in Angus with critical intervals of need

Estimated range (number)	2599 – 1531
Range (per 1,000 population)	321 – 189

Service per 1,000 population 75+	Angus Rate per 1,000 population 75+	Scotland Rate per 1,000 population 75+
Long-stay care beds[1]	20.2	36.4
Psychogeriatric beds[1]	124.2	33.7
Total hospital beds	144.4	70.1
Places in residential homes[2]	73.5	53.2
Places in nursing homes[2]	66.8	69.4
Very sheltered housing[3]	0.0	
Total residential homes, nursing homes, very sheltered housing	140.3	109.8
Social care officer	not known	
6/7 day home help[4]	34.2	25.6
Total units of support	318.9	218.2

1 Source: Tables 11 & 4 (p.180), Angus Community Care Plan, (figures for March 1995)

2 Source: Table 2e, Vacancy Monitoring Report, SWSG (figures for March 1996)

3 Source: Table 8, Angus Community Care Plan, (figures for March 1995)

4 Source: Table 9.8 Community Care Bulletin, SWSG, (figures for March 1995)

The table indicates that between 321 and 189 people, in every 1,000 members of the population aged 75+, have critical intervals of need and require intensive levels of support. For this population there are 144 places in hospital, 140 in residential and nursing homes and some 34 people, living at home, receiving the home help service 6/7 days a week..

When comparing provision of services with the Scottish average, Angus has higher than average places in hospital, residential and nursing homes.

The figure Total "units of support" of 318.9 suggests that there is sufficient provision, overall, for older people with critical intervals of need in Angus. However, that support is very much within hospital, residential or nursing homes. Angus has relatively little provision for people at home.

Notes to Spreadsheet "Intervals of need."

- **Population:** these are mid-year 1994, with the "L(iving)Alone" figures taken from the 1991 Census.

- **Critical interval**

The population of chair or bed bound people is derived from adding the prevalence rates of people who are unable to get out of bed or a chair unaided (for both all 75+, and 75+ living alone) of the GHS Survey to the relevant numbers of older people living in communal establishments. The figure for those in residential and nursing homes is derived from Table 2.14 of the SWSG Community Care Bulletin figures for March 1995 and Table 6d-2 ISD, 1995, using 'physical disability' as a proxy. For this exercise all older people in communal establishments are counted as living alone. In this sub-table there is no allowance made for the number of 75+ in hospital, who are chair or bed bound.

Data on incontinence within the community is sparse. In this exercise the number of people in the community was calculated from Campbell et al (1985), for both all 75+, and 75+ living alone. This was added to the numbers of older people in communal establishments estimated to be incontinent. Again all those in communal establishments were reckoned to live alone. In this sub-table there is no allowance made for the number of 75+ in hospital, who are incontinent.

The work of Jorm, Korten and Henderson is used to provide the prevalence data for all people 75+ with dementia, including those living in communal establishments. The data on people with dementia who live alone is derived from the Forth Valley Health Board survey which contains an analysis of the place of residence of people with dementia, and how many live alone. The population of those living alone was computed by adding those in communal establishments to 11% of the Jorm, Korten and Henderson population.

- **Short and long intervals**

For this exercise all older people who are unable to cook a main meal (short interval) or need help with one or more domestic task (long interval) are assumed to be living at home, rather than in communal establishments. It is also assumed that all people who have short intervals of need also have long intervals. Hence the numbers of people with short intervals of need are deducted (in the authority's summary) from the number with long intervals. If that need is met, time wise, other, longer interval needs can also be met by definition.

"ANGUS, DUNDEE PERTH & KINROSS INSPECTION NEEDS ASSESSMENT"

INTERVALS OF NEED

OLDER PEOPLE 75+

"POPULATION, Mid-year 1994 (from profiles)"

	75-84 All	75-84 LAlone*	85+ All	85+ LAlone*	Total 75+	Total 75+ LAlone	% Living Alone
Angus	5986	2563	2118	633	**8104**	**3196**	39%
Dundee	7567	4730	2416	1210	**9983**	**5940**	60%
P&K	7720	3455	2506	871	**10226**	**4326**	42%
Total	21273	10748	7040	2714	28313	13462	

* figures from 1991 census

CRITICAL INTERVAL

1.1 All older people - Chair/bed bound — Proxies for physical disability

"[GHS, Table 31 Getting in/out of bed - community + homes]" — RHs - Table 2.14 / NHs - Table 6d-2

	Total 75+	**2%**	Number	38%	Number	71%	Total
Angus	8104	**162**	557	212	335	238	**612**
Dundee	9983	**200**	779	296	521	370	**866**
P&K	10226	**205**	858	326	653	464	**995**
Total	28313	566	2194	834	1509	1071	

1.2 Older people, living alone - Chair/bed bound — Proxies for physical disability

"[GHS, Table 31 Getting in/out of bed - community + homes]" — RHs - Table 2.14 / NHs - Table 6d-2

	Total 75+	**1%**	Number	38%	Number	71%	Total
Angus	8104	**81**	557	212	335	238	**531**
Dundee	9983	**100**	779	296	521	370	**766**
P&K	10226	**102**	858	326	653	464	**892**
Total	28313	135	2194	834	1509	1071	2040

2. Incontinence "[Tables 2.14,SWSG, 6d -2, ISD]"

	RH Beds	19%	NH Beds	19%	11% Campbell	**2.1 All older p.**	% Living al.	Number L.Alone	**2.2 Old.people living alone**
Angus	557	106	335	64	891	1061	39%	348	517
Dundee	779	148	521	99	1098	1345	60%	659	906
P&K	858	163	653	124	1125	1412	42%	472	760
	2194	417	1509	287	3114	3818	1479	2183	

3.1 All older people - dementia

"[Application of Jorm,Korten and Henderson studies of dementia prevalence (applying population distribution of 1992)]"

		75-79	**5.60%**	**80-84**	**10.50%**	**85-89**	**20.80%**	**90+**	**38.60%**	**Total**	
Angus	8104	3809	213	2593	272	1216	253	486	188	8842	**926**
Dundee	9983	4692	263	3195	335	1497	311	599	231	10893	**1141**
P&K	10226	4806	269	3272	344	1534	319	614	237	11158	**1169**
Total	28313	13307	745	9060	951	4247	883	1699	656	30893	3236

3.2 Older people living alone - dementia

[Application of Forth Valley Health Board data]

			M/stream 47%	Shelt.Hsing 8%	RHs 12%	NHs 15%	Ger.CC 13%	Psyc.CC 7%	Live alone 11%	Communal Establish.	
Angus		**926**	435	74	111	139	120	65	48	435	**483**
Dundee		**1141**	536	91	137	171	148	80	59	536	**595**
P&K		**1169**	549	94	140	175	152	82	60	549	**610**
	3236	1520	259	388	485	421	227	167	1521	1688	

SHORT INTERVAL "[GHS, Table 45, Cook a main meal]"

1. All older people			**"2. Older people, living alone"**	
	Total 75+	**11%**	**Total 75+**	**7%**
Angus	8104	**891**	3196	**224**
Dundee	9983	**1098**	5940	**416**
P&K	10226	**1125**	4326	**303**
Total	28313	3114	13462	942

LONG INTERVAL "[GHS, Table 47, Needing help with one or more domestic care task]"

1. All older people			**"2. Older people, living alone"**	
	Total 75+	**38%**	**Total 75+**	**39%**
Angus	8104	**3080**	3196	**1246**
Dundee	9983	**3794**	5940	**2317**
P&K	10226	**3886**	4326	**1687**
Total	28313	10759	13462	5250

Appendix 2

Notes To Costs Analysis

Background to Costings

We were informed by the Councils that the figures submitted were extracted from the 1996/97 budget allocation. To these figures we added a 6% cost of Capital (per CIPFA guidance). A depreciation charge based on an estimated remaining life of 25 years (agreed with the Council) was added to the figures supplied by Angus Council and Dundee City Council, as it was those Councils' view that repairs and maintenance were insufficient to prevent a permanent diminution in the value of the properties. No such additional charge was made in relation to Perth & Kinross where repairs and maintenance were considered by the Council to be sufficient to prevent depreciation.

Income received by the homes was excluded, as this was minimal, in order to reflect the gross cost to the Council of providing the service.

In Dundee, the number of long term residents and the number of care days were both taken as the number as at 31 May 1996. The Council has confirmed that, for both types of care, these figures are representative of normal activity. In Angus the number of long-term residents and number of care days used for calculation purposes were based on the average weekly numbers of older people receiving care between April and September 1996. In Perth & Kinross, calculations were based on average weekly numbers of older people receiving care between April and August 1996.

The costs of older people receiving respite care in local authority residential homes was excluded in Dundee and in Perth & Kinross, where the councils considered that this had only a small marginal cost effect. We have included respite care costs in our figures for Angus, since we were advised that the Council apportions specific costs to this service.

The separation of older people into age categories was based on statistical information supplied by the Social Work Services Group.

Finally, the level of income support premiums noted in the calculation was provided by the Department of Social Security.

The band estimates of the overall potential savings were calculated as follows. We estimated the maximum long term saving if all the councils homes were closed or transferred by subtracting from the average unit cost the elements for overheads (recharges) and one third of the capital costs (which would not be saved). This figure was multiplied by the average number of residents and that figure by 52 to reach a maximum long-term annual saving. Potential savings could be reduced by several factors such as redundancy costs, potential increases in prices, the cost of including more single rooms etc.

It is not possible to calculate these factors at this stage. In addition there are arguments for each authority to retain some provision. The lower band figure was therefore calculated by halving the figure for the average number of residents. This provides for the potential effects of several factors and should not be taken to imply that the only factor involved would be the number of beds closed.

Note 1

The Premiums paid are dependent upon the age of the resident. Social Work Services Group supplied us with the following Income Support premiums and estimated spread of residential care population within Angus. The £23.23 is the weighted average of these premiums as follows :

Age	Premium £	Percentage of Population %	Average Premium £
65-75	19.15	13	2.49
75-80	21.30	39	8.31
>80	25.90	48	12.43
			23.23

Note 2

Figures submitted by the 3 local authorities to us show that 95% of local authority residential home residents in Angus, 98% in Dundee and 90.5% in Perth & Kinross, are local authority financed. These individuals are in receipt of income support at the following rates : £61.75 per week for a local authority resident and £47.90 per week for an independent home resident. Of these amounts, £13.75 is retained by the individual resident.

Appendix 3

Local Authority Costings

LOCAL AUTHORITY RESIDENTIAL – ANGUS (All Residents)

Name of Home EXPENDITURE	A £	%	B £	%	C £	%	D £	%	E £	%	F £	%
Staff costs	434,079	74.0	376,750	74.4	437,664	68.3	390,755	72.6	333,789	74.9	670,725	77.1
Premises	14,000	2.4	15,000	3.0	22,000	3.4	17,000	3.2	12,000	2.7	19,500	2.2
Supplies & Services	39,000	6.6	34,000	6.7	58,000	9.1	40,000	7.4	30,000	6.7	72,000	8.3
Depreciation	22,320	3.8	16,848	3.3	30,456	4.8	20,088	3.7	5,100	1.1	0	0.0
Cost of capital	33,480	5.7	25,272	5.0	45,684	7.1	30,132	5.6	30,600	6.9	38,880	4.5
Support Costs*	27,910	4.8	24,395	4.8	29,874	4.7	25,656	4.8	21,533	4.8	43,675	5.0
Recharges*	16,025	2.7	14,007	2.8	17,038	2.7	14,731	2.7	12,363	2.8	25,077	2.9
Transport	0	0.0	0	0.0	0	0.0	0	0.0	0	0.0	0	0.0
Total Expenditure	586,814	100.0	506,272	100.0	640,716	100.0	538,362	100.0	445,385	100.0	869,857	100.0
Gross Expenditure	586,814		506,272		640,716		538,362		445,385		869,857	
Average Number of Residents April – Sept '96	24		24		29		23		14		46	
Cost/resident/week	470.20		405.67		424.88		450.14		611.79		363.65	

* support costs based on 5.7% of staff costs, Premises and Supplies and Services.
* Recharges based on 3.29% of staff costs, Premises and Supplies and Services.

LOCAL AUTHORITY RESIDENTIAL – ANGUS (Non-Dementia)

Name of Home EXPENDITURE	A £	%	B £	%	C £	%	D £	%	E £	%	F £	%
Staff costs	217,039	69.5	376,750	74.4	437,664	68.3	390,755	72.6	333,789	74.9	471.992	75.0
Premises	9,333	3.0	15,000	3.0	22,000	3.4	17,000	3.2	12,000	2.7	16,109	2.6
Supplies & Services	26,000	8.3	34,000	6.7	58,000	9.1	40,000	7.4	30,000	6.7	59,478	9.5
Depreciation	14,880	4.8	16,848	3.3	30,456	4.8	20,088	3.7	5,100	1.1	0	0.0
Cost of capital	22,320	7.1	25,272	5.0	45,684	7.1	30,132	5.6	30,600	6.9	32,118	5.1
Support Costs*	14,461	4.6	24,395	4.8	29,874	4.7	25,656	4.8	21,533	4.8	31,376	5.0
Recharges*	8,303	2.7	14,007	2.8	17,038	2.7	14,731	2.7	12,363	2.8	18,015	2.9
Transport	0	0.0	0	0.0	0	0.0	0	0.0	0	0.0	0	0.0
Total Expenditure	312,336	100.0	506,272	100.0	640,716	100.0	538,362	100.0	445,385	100.0	629,088	100.0
Gross Expenditure	312,336		506,272		640,716		538,362		445,385		629,088	
Average Number of Residents April – Sept '96	16		24		29		23		14		38	
Cost/resident/week	375.40		405.67		424.88		450.14		611.79		318.36	

* support costs based on 5.7% of staff costs, Premises and Supplies and Services.
* Recharges based on 3.29% of staff costs, Premises and Supplies and Services.
* The costs for homes "A" and "F" have been reduced to remove costs associated with providing Dementia Care

LOCAL AUTHORITY RESIDENTIAL – ANGUS (Dementia)

Name of Home	A		F	
EXPENDITURE	£	%	£	%
Staff costs	217,039	79.1	196,733	81.7
Premises	4,667	1.7	3,391	1.4
Supplies & Services	13,000	4.7	12,522	5.2
Depreciation	7,440	2.7	0	0.0
Cost of capital	11,160	4.1	8,762	3.6
Support Costs*	13,449	4.9	12,299	5.1
Recharges*	7,722	2.8	7,062	2.9
Transport	0	0.0	0	0.0
Total Expenditure	274,477	100.0	240,769	100.0
Gross Expenditure	274,477		240,769	
Average Number of Residents April – Sept '96	8		8	
Cost/resident/week	659.80		578.77	

* support costs based on 5.7% of staff costs, Premises and Supplies and Services.
* Recharges based on 3.29% of staff costs, Premises and Supplies and Services.

LOCAL AUTHORITY DAY CARE – ANGUS

Name of Home	F	
EXPENDITURE	£	%
Staff costs	78,439	73.4
Premises	6,500	6.1
Supplies & Services	0	0.0
Depreciation	0	0.0
Cost of capital	12,960	12.1
Support Costs	5,000	4.7
Transport	4,000	3.7
Total Expenditure	106,899	100.0
Net Expenditure	106,899	
Number of care days per week at 31/5	67 (actual attendance) (available – 84)	
Cost/care day	30.68	

LOCAL AUTHORITY DOMICILIARY CARE– ANGUS

EXPENDITURE	£	%
Staff costs	2,543,000	92.7
Premises	5,000	0.2
Supplies & Services	14,000	0.5
Depreciation	2,000	0.1
Support Costs	0	0.0
Transport	178,000	6.5
Other Operational Costs	0	0.0
Total Expenditure	2,742,000	100.0
INCOME		
Charges	0	
Grant Income	0	
Miscellaneous	0	
Total Income	0	
Net Expenditure	2,742,000	
Number of hours per week at 31/5	8,431	
Cost to the Authority/ care hour	6.25	

LOCAL AUTHORITY RESIDENTIAL – DUNDEE

Name of Home	A		B		C		D		E		F		G		H		I	
EXPENDITURE	£	%	£	%	£	%	£	%	£	%	£	%	£	%	£	%	£	%
Staff costs	386,305	73.0	560,142	74.5	468,100	73.9	419,375	74.6	554,826	72.9	480,281	73.8	535,003	74.4	494,510	74.2	469,317	74.4
Premises	1,394	0.3	1,828	0.2	2,252	0.4	1,606	0.3	2,247	0.3	2,470	0.4	1,663	0.2	1,825	0.3	2,397	0.4
Supplies & Services	28,093	5.3	45,334	6.0	38,404	6.1	30,657	5.5	45,334	6.0	40,156	6.2	41,869	5.8	41,860	6.3	38,414	6.1
Depreciation	8,330	1.6	10,637	1.4	9,097	1.4	7,057	1.3	28,345	3.7	8,632	1.3	19,554	2.7	9,499	1.4	7,947	1.3
Cost of capital	31,104	5.9	51,840	6.9	38,880	6.1	30,132	5.4	46,656	6.1	39,852	6.1	39,744	5.5	39,852	6.0	38,880	6.2
Support Costs*	30,673	5.8	20,008	2.7	22,352	3.5	25.143	4.5	20,210	2.7	22,970	3.5	19,444	2.7	21,144	3.2	20,712	3.3
Recharges*	43,487	8.21	61,807	8.22	54,230	8.56	47,888	8.52	63,028		56,547		61,501		58,000		53,261	
Transport	0	0.0	0	0.0	0	0.0	0	0.0	0	0.0	0	0.0	0	0.0	0	0.0	0	0.0
Total Expenditure	529,386	100.0	751,596	100.0	633,315	100.0	561,858	100.0	760,646	100.0	650,908	100.0	718,778	100.0	666,690	100.0	630,928	100.0
Gross Expenditure	529,386		751,596		633,315		561,858		760,646		650,908		718,778		666,690		630,928	
Number of long term Residents at 31/5	28		48		40		31		46		43		44		43		40	
Cost/long term resident/week	363.59		301.12		304.48		348.55		318.00		291.10		314.15		298.16		303.33	

* based on budgets.

LOCAL AUTHORITY DAY CARE – DUNDEE

Name of Home	I		G	
EXPENDITURE	£	%	£	%
Staff costs	301,103	66.4	137,245	67.4
Premises	830	0.2	447	0.2
Supplies & Services	20,683	4.6	20,328	10.0
Depreciation	12,519	2.8	5,261	2.6
Cost of capital	15,126		9,936	4.9
Support Costs	10,856	2.4	5,231	2.6
Recharges	70,365	15.5	20,530	10.1
Transport	21,893	4.8	4,506	2.2
Total Expenditure	453,375	100.0	203,484	100.0
INCOME				
Telephone	0		0	
Charges	0		0	
Miscellaneous	8,995		0	
Total Income	8,995		0	
Net Expenditure	444,380		203,484	
Number of care days per week at 31/5	246		99	
Cost/care day	34.74		39.53	

LOCAL AUTHORITY DOMICILIARY CARE – DUNDEE

EXPENDITURE	£	%
Staff costs	4,574,945	95.8
Premises	10,579	0.2
Supplies & Services	46,986	1.0
Support Costs	12,216	0.3
Transport	128,475	2.7
Other Operational Costs	0	0.0
Total Expenditure	4,773,201	100.0
INCOME		
Charges	0	
Grant Income	0	
Miscellaneous	0	
Total Income	0	
Net Expenditure	4,773,201	
Number of hours per week at 31/5	14,900	
Cost to the LA/care hour	6.16	

LOCAL AUTHORITY RESIDENTIAL – PERTH & KINROSS

Name of Home	A		B		C		D	
EXPENDITURE	£	%	£	%	£	%	£	%
Staff costs	474,032	68.8	566,694	70.4	426,058	68.4	472,841	66.4
Premises	33,865	4.9	30,060	3.7	39,125	6.3	59,282	8.3
Supplies & Services	55,300	8.0	54,772	6.8	43,174	6.9	54,284	7.6
Cost of capital	47,520	6.9	56,160	7.0	32,640	5.2	38,400	5.4
Support Costs*	16,247	2.4	23,481	2.9	25,139	4.0	22,462	3.2
Recharges*	58,314	8.5	68,089	8.5	53,655	8.6	61,232	8.6
Transport	3,700	0.5	5,880	0.7	3,050	0.5	3,450	0.5
Total Expenditure	688,978	100.0	805,136	100.0	622,841	100.0	711,951	100.0
Number of long term Residents average, over April-August	35		46		30		34	
Cost/long term resident/week	378.56		336.60		399.26		402.69	

No Depreciation on Homes due to high repairs and maintenance costs.

* support costs (budgeted expenditure).
* Recharges (10% of relevant expenditure).

CHURCH OF SCOTLAND – RESIDENTIAL

	Dementia Unit		Very Sheltered Housing	
EXPENDITURE	£	%	£	%
Staff costs	160,373	79.5	287,309	75.9
Premises	2,100	1.0	4,900	1.3
Supplies & Services	11,230	5.6	26,120	6.9
Repairs & Maintenance	5,970	3.0	13,870	3.7
Cost of capital	0	0.0	0	0.0
Support Costs	11,310	5.6	21,700	5.7
Recharged Services	10,630	5.3	24,790	6.5
Total Expenditure	201,613	100.0	378,689	100.0
Income	67,613		210,689	
Net Expenditure	134,000		168,000	
Number of long term Residents	8		18	
Cost/long term resident/week	322.12		179.49	

LOCAL AUTHORITY DAY CARE – PERTH & KINROSS

Name of Home	F		B		C		D	
EXPENDITURE	£	%	£	%	£	%	£	%
Staff costs	328,600	75.7	105,406	88.4	9,642	90.4	9,642	90.4
Premises	17,099	3.9	3,420	2.9	0	0.0	0	0.0
Supplies & Services	31,490	7.3	6,298	5.3	1,026	9.6	1,026	9.6
Support Costs	11,728	2.7	460	0.4	0	0.0	0	0.0
Cost of Capital	27,000	0.1						
Transport	18,100	4.2	3,620	3.0	0	0.0	0	0.0
Total Expenditure	434,017	100.0	119,204	100.0	10,668	100.0	10,668	100.0
Number of care days per week avg April-Aug	247		38		6		24	
Cost/care day	33.79		60.33		34.19		8.55	

LOCAL AUTHORITY DOMICILIARY CARE – PERTH & KINROSS

EXPENDITURE	£	%
Staff costs	2,515,650	89.5
Premises	3,900	0.1
Supplies & Services	49,500	1.8
Support Costs	10,394	0.4
Overhead	0	0.0
Transport	232,850	8.3
Total Expenditure	2,812,294	100.0
Number of hours per week at 31/5	8,551	
Cost to the LA/care hour	6.32	

No depreciation due to
Repairs and maintenance costs.

Appendix 4

The Quality Of Care In Residential Care Homes And Nursing Homes

The legislative context

Setting standards for the quality of care of older people living in long stay settings and monitoring adherence to those standards is currently the responsibility of local authority social work departments or health boards, depending on whether social or nursing care is provided.

Residential Care Homes are registered under the 1968 Social Work (Scotland) Act as amended by the 1987 Registered Establishments (Scotland) Act and the National Health Service and Community Care Act (1990). Under the NHS and Community Care Act (1990) local authorities set up separate, 'arm's length' units to carry out at least one comprehensive annual inspection of all registered residential care homes, including their own. These units have been in place since 1 April 1990. With the reorganisation of local government into 32 unitary authorities in April 1996, some authorities have collaborated in establishing joint social work inspection units to enable consistency of approach and standards and cost-effective use of staff. However, Angus, Dundee and Perth & Kinross Councils have opted to set up their own individual inspection units. Section 5 of the 1987 Act provides for joint registration with local authorities and Health Boards of establishments wishing to provide both social work residential and nursing home care. At present, there are just two such establishments operating in the Tayside Health Board area.

Nursing Homes are registered with Health Boards under the 1938 Nursing Homes Registration (Scotland) Act and are inspected by officers from inspection units of these Boards. Most local authority Inspection Units have developed working relationships with Health Board Inspection Units. Some are collaborating to produce joint registration guidelines within the limits of the different legislation and care requirements. Others are developing common standards for both residential and nursing homes and in a few areas, joint visits and contributions to each others' inspection reports are taking place.

Standard-setting in residential care homes

The responsibility for setting standards in residential care homes lies with the individual local authority, in consultation with the key organisations and individuals who will be affected by them. Under the Citizen's Charter, service standards are expected to be realistic, attainable, challenging and reflecting users' needs. They should be regularly monitored and published, and progressively raised. In residential care, standards should address the desired quality of life of people living in homes.

A Standards document for residential care homes was developed by the inspection unit of the former Tayside Region and agreed by Tayside Regional Council in 1993, with the expectation that these standards would be adopted by the new Councils after April 1996. A revised version of the Standards and Guidance for Good Practice was out for consultation with the Directors of the three Unitary Councils at the time of the Scottish Office inspection. Inspection units reach their conclusions about the quality of care provided on the basis of personal observation during inspection visits, through interviews with a sample quarter of a home's residents, by consulting samples of written records and through discussion with home managers or owners. We examined the reports available on the most recently conducted annual inspections in residential homes for older people. Some of these reports relate to inspections carried out by the inspection unit of Tayside Regional Council, others, carried out since 1 April 1996, have been conducted by the new inspection units of the three individual Councils in Angus, Dundee and Perth & Kinross..

Our Analysis of Inspection Reports by the Local Authorities and Tayside Health Board

The number of standards in each category under which homes were inspected varied within and between authorities over time. The inspection took an average of the number of standards applied across the three Councils and used it as a base for comparing how well homes did or did not meet these standards. The greatest number of standards were in the section labelled 'Functions and Objectives' - a maximum of 113 different indicators by which a home's functions and objectives were judged. By contrast, the 'Staffing' standards numbered a maximum of 36. This was taken into account when calculating average numbers of standards applied overall. If these standards are a reliable indicator of quality in residential care homes, the general level of compliance is high. However, some standards have potentially much greater implications for a resident's quality of life than others. For example, whether all residents sharing a bedroom are doing so by choice does not have a greater numerical value than whether they have signed their care plan, although it is likely that inspectors will place greater value on the former standard being met. Our analysis has been applied to homes by sector and did not apply weightings to individual standards. The resulting analysis is, therefore, somewhat crude as a result and the standards applied have been taken as proxy indicators of quality of care. Given these limitations, the picture that emerges is generally positive.

We based our conclusions about quality in nursing homes on reports of recently completed inspections carried out by Health Board inspection staff. Nursing home inspections are carried out by a team of officers consisting of a nurse, medical officer and pharmacist, each of whom takes discrete responsibility for an area of the inspection. Information is collected about home and patient records, staffing, services provided, medical and surgical supplies, catering and accommodation for residents and for staff. The overall impression gained during the inspection about the state of repair, decoration and cleanliness of the home is noted, as is a summary of the overall well-being and appearance of patients/residents. It was not clear from the reports that residents' views were invariably sought during inspections.

Notes

1 Scottish Office Statistical Bulletin 1995

2 Scottish Health Statistics, ISD, 1995

3 Social care officers are staff employed on residential conditions of service, working flexible hours and with a remuneration that recognises a wider range of personal care tasks, compared to home helps

4 "Caring for People", HMSO 1989

5 Tobin, S S and Lieberman, MA (1976) "Last Home for the Aged." California: Jossey-Bass. Yawney, BA and Slover, DL (1973) "Relocation of the Elderly" Social Work 18(3): pages 86-95

6 "The Measurement of Need in Older People", Scottish Health Services Studies, Scottish Home and Health Department, 1976.

7 "Population Needs Assessment in Community Care", Social Work Services Inspectorate, HMSO, 1996.

8 Scottish Office Statistical Bulletin 1995

9 Petch A, Cheetham J, Fuller R, MacDonald C and Myers F with Hallam Aand Knapp M, (1996) "Delivering Community Care. Initial Implementation of Care Management in Scotland" HMSO,

10 Social Work Services Group, 'Vacancy Monitoring Report July 1996'; unpublished.

11 See Appendix 1, "Matching the Needs of, and Provision for, Older People aged 75+"

12 A "unit of support" is a response to the help or assistance required by an individual, e.g. a hospital bed, a very sheltered housing flatlet, a home help service, etc.

13 See Appendix 2 Notes to Costs Analysis

14 See Appendix 2 Notes to Costs Analysis

15 See Appendix 2 Notes to Costs Analysis

16 See Appendix 1 "Matching the Needs of, and Provision for Older People aged 75+"

17 A "unit of support" is a response to the help or assistance required by an individual, e.g. a hospital bed, a very sheltered housing flatlet , a home help service, etc.

18 Both Strathmore House and Pinegrove were excluded from this analysis. Strathmore House closed in July 1996, and Pinegrove closed in June 1996.

19 See Appendix 2 Notes to Costs Analysis

20 See Appendix 2 Notes to Costs Analysis

21 See Appendix 2 Notes to Costs Analysis

22 See Appendix 1, "Matching the Needs of, and Provision for , Older People aged 75+"

23 A "unit of support" is a response to the needs of an individual, e.g. a hospital bed, a very sheltered housing flatlet, the home help service, etc.

24 Source: SWSG Statistical Branch, Vacancy Monitoring Report. July 1996

25 See Appendix 2 Notes to Costs Analysis

26 See Appendix 2 Notes to Costs Analysis

27 See Appendix 2 Notes to Costs Analysis

28 Sinclair, Ian (1988) Residential Care: The Research Reviewed, National Institute for Social Work.
Willcocks D., Peace S., and Kellaher L., (1987) Private Lives in Public Places. Tavistock Publications

29 Residential Care Home Registration Procedures, SWSG, June 1996

30 SW13/1994, Community Care Plans: Direction on Purchasing, SWSG, 2 November 1994

31 Squaring the Circle, Managing Community Care Resources, Accounts Commission, September 1994

32 Squaring the Circle, Managing Community Care Resources, Accounts Commission, September 1994

33 Squaring the Circle, Managing Community Care Resources, Accounts Commission, September 1994

34 Hardy Brian, Young Ruth and Wistow Gerald, Purchasing Domiciliary Care: The Provider Perspective Nuffield Institute for Health, October 1996

35 GHS Survey 1991, People aged 65 and over, OPCS, 1995